HUG[illegible]

Just brilliant. Learner's Permit Guides make dense topics accessible.

— PHILIP VON DIRKSEN

Essential reading for anyone trying to understand the intellectual currents shaping Silicon Valley's vision of governance. Clear-eyed and measured.

— JAMES REYNOLDS

Finally, a systematic analysis that neither sensationalizes nor dismisses these challenging ideas. Essential for understanding the philosophical roots of modern techno-libertarianism.

— RACHEL CHEN

Curtis Yarvin & The Neoreactionary Canon, Made Simple

Curtis Yarvin & The Neoreactionary Canon, Made Simple

Learner's Permit Guide

Book Two

Hugo Thornton Rowley

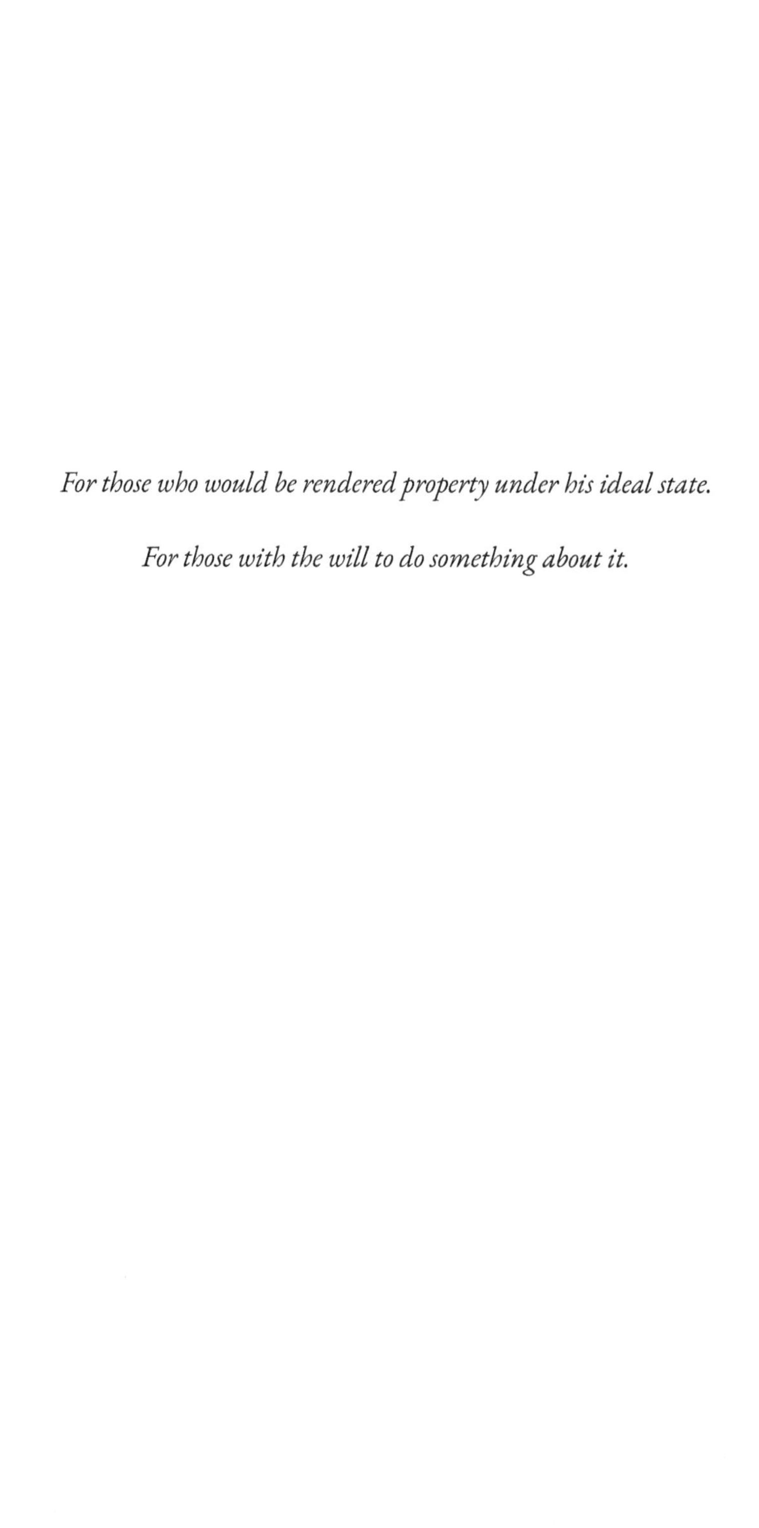

For those who would be rendered property under his ideal state.

For those with the will to do something about it.

The surest way to work up a crusade in favor of some good cause is to promise people they will have a chance of maltreating someone. To be able to destroy with good conscience, to be able to behave badly and call your bad behavior 'righteous indignation' — this is the height of psychological luxury, the most delicious of moral treats.

— Aldous Huxley

A Learner's Permit for Neoreactionary Canon

This book serves as a structured guide to the *Neoreactionary Canon* and the work of Curtis Yarvin. The *Canon* is a collection of blog posts and essays from figures within the neoreactionary movement, an intellectual current that **critiques democracy, egalitarianism, and modern liberalism in favor of hierarchical governance, technocratic rule, and authoritarian stability.**

Yarvin, formerly writing under the pseudonym Mencius Moldbug, is a highly controversial political thinker. His work has inspired tech elites, reactionary intellectuals, and radical political movements alike. But what exactly does he argue? How do his ideas connect? And where, if at all, do his arguments fall apart?

This guide distills the key ideas of *Neoreactionary Canon* and Yarvin, providing an in-depth overview of his core concepts, rhetorical strategies, and historical claims. It presents his arguments without distortion but also scrutinizes where he refines his rhetoric to obscure controversial conclusions, selectively interprets history, or relies on flawed assumptions.

WHAT IS NEOREACTION?

Neoreaction, often abbreviated as **NRx,** is a loosely connected set of **political theories that reject democracy, egalitarianism, and modern liberal governance in favor of hierarchy, authoritarianism, and centralized rule.** Its most famous proponent, Curtis Yarvin, argues that democracy is inherently corrupt, progressivism is a religious-like ideology, and governance should be structured like a corporate monarchy.

WHO IS CURTIS YARVIN, AND WHY DOES HE MATTER?

Yarvin is not a mainstream political theorist. He does not belong to an established academic school of thought. His work is not cited in traditional policy circles. And yet, his ideas have had a profound influence on certain sectors of Silicon Valley, the dissident right, and political circles advocating for alternatives to democracy.

In 2007 he began publishing sprawling blog posts that blended history, political theory, and software engineering metaphors.

His central argument is straightforward:

1. Democracy is a failed system.
2. It is inefficient, unstable, and deceptive, giving the illusion of public control.
3. Real power lies with a permanent bureaucratic and intellectual class he calls "The Cathedral."
4. His proposed alternative is a monarchy-like

corporate state, governed by a CEO rather than elected politicians.

While this sounds extreme, his influence is undeniable:

- Peter Thiel, the billionaire venture capitalist, has publicly echoed Yarvin's ideas, arguing that democracy and capitalism are in conflict.
- JD Vance, a Vice President of the United States, has similarly referenced Yarvin's work.
- Yarvin's "Cathedral" framework has become a popular way to critique progressive cultural hegemony, even outside neoreactionary circles.
  His ideas on governance overlap with the techno-libertarian push for private cities, "exit" from failing states, and governance-as-a-service models.
- These theories echo those outlined in *The Sovereign Individual* by Rees-Mogg and Davidson - another influential work for those who wish to move away from democracy, the nation-state and fiat currency.

Yarvin is not just a radical political thinker, he is also a rhetorician. Over time, he has refined his messaging to appeal to different audiences. His early writings spoke openly of monarchy, but as this alienated some readers, he began using corporate governance metaphors instead (replacing "king" with "CEO"). This is not a shift in ideology but a strategic rebranding - a recurring pattern in his work.

The Aim of the Learner's Permit

This guide serves three purposes. First, it summarizes and distills Yarvin's most important arguments, removing unnecessary digressions. Second, it organizes his thoughts into a structured, readable format. Third, it provides critical analysis that identifies where he stretches history, refines his rhetoric, or contradicts himself.

Each chapter follows a consistent format. We begin with "What Yarvin Argues," providing a clear, neutral summary of his position. This is followed by a "Critical Response" that analyzes his claims, highlighting flaws in reasoning or historical inaccuracies. For example, when Yarvin claims universal suffrage has led to societal decline, we summarize his reasoning, examine historical counterexamples where expanded voting rights led to stability and growth, and highlight his rhetorical strategy, such as his tendency to frame democracy's failures as inevitable while downplaying historical failures of authoritarianism.

Key Themes in Yarvin's Work

The Cathedral and the Hidden Power Structure is central to Yarvin's thought. He argues that power in modern society is not held by elected officials but by an interconnected elite of journalists, academics, and bureaucrats who shape public opinion. He likens it to a decentralized theocracy, where ideological conformity is enforced through cultural and institutional pressure rather than legal means.

The Failure of Democracy is another key theme. Democracy, he claims, is a chaotic, short-termist system that incentivizes corruption and decay. He contrasts this with monarchy (or its rebranded form, a corporate-run state), which he argues is more stable and efficient.

Exit Over Voice represents his solution. Instead of political participation ("voice"), Yarvin argues for "exit" - leaving failed democratic systems and forming new, efficient microstates, private cities, or corporate-governed societies.

Who Should Read This?

This guide is for anyone seeking to understand neoreactionary thought and its influence on contemporary politics and technology. You don't need to agree with Yarvin to find his ideas worth understanding - they have shaped significant currents in modern political and technological discourse.

How to Use This Book

The chapters cover major aspects of *Neoreactionary Canon* including:

- The Cathedral (Yarvin's theory of hidden power)
- Democracy's Supposed Failures (his argument against democracy)
- Neocameralism (his CEO-state alternative)
- Race, Gender, and Hierarchy (his views on social structure)
- Exit vs. Voice (why he believes political reform is pointless)
- Historical Revisionism (how he uses history to justify reactionary positions)
- Yarvin's Influence Today (how his ideas have shaped modern right-wing thought).

Each chapter is self-contained, so you can read them in any order based on your interests.

Understanding Yarvin Without Mythologizing Him

Yarvin is often treated as either a political prophet or a dangerous extremist. This guide takes neither position.

Instead, it aims to present his work accurately, highlighting both his intellectual contributions and his rhetorical manipulations.

Let's get into it.

Yarvin's Rhetorical Strategies

Curtis Yarvin is not just a political theorist - he is, first and foremost, a rhetorician. His writing is marked by a distinctive style: sprawling essays filled with historical metaphors, technical jargon, and provocative claims wrapped in an air of intellectual detachment. But beneath the wordplay and literary references lies a carefully crafted effort to **make radical ideas sound reasonable.**

Yarvin's influence does not stem from original political thought - most of his core ideas are rehashed reactionary talking points repackaged for the tech age. Instead, his power comes from his ability to frame these ideas in ways that appeal to different audiences while maintaining plausible deniability about their more extreme implications.

His rhetorical strategies can be broken down into several key techniques: **reframing authoritarianism as governance optimization, leveraging historical metaphors, strategic ambiguity, audience segmentation, and the gradual radicalization of the reader**.

REBRANDING AUTHORITARIANISM AS A "MODERN" SOLUTION

Yarvin's most effective rhetorical move is presenting monarchy, dictatorship, and elite rule not as outdated relics but as *superior governance models.* He avoids traditional authoritarian language in favor of terms borrowed from business, technology, and engineering.

For example:

- Instead of "monarchy," he proposes **"neocameralism"** - a system where the state is run like a corporation with a sovereign CEO.
- Instead of referring to democracy's failure in moral or ideological terms, he presents it as a **"bad operating system"** - a defective piece of software that should be replaced.
- Instead of openly advocating for dictatorship, he argues for **"patching and upgrading" governance** as if it were merely a technical issue.

This rhetorical approach serves two purposes:

1. **It makes authoritarianism sound pragmatic, rather than ideological** - something that can be justified on efficiency grounds rather than as a moral or historical necessity.
2. **It makes his arguments more appealing to Silicon Valley audiences**, many of whom are comfortable with corporate hierarchy and see governance as a problem to be "solved" through systems design rather than politics.

The Strategic Swap: Kings Become CEOs

One of Yarvin's most transparent rhetorical shifts over time has been his rebranding of kings and absolute rulers as *sovereign executives*. His early writing openly advocated for monarchy, using historical figures like Frederick the Great and Louis XIV as examples. But as he realized that advocating for kings was alienating potential followers, he began using corporate analogies instead.

This was not a change in ideology, but a **change in branding**. Instead of kings ruling by divine right, his new model suggests they rule as shareholders overseeing a national enterprise. But **functionally, the system remains the same: absolute power in the hands of a single individual.**

Historical Metaphors and the Illusion of Inevitable Decline

Yarvin frequently frames his arguments using **long historical narratives** - not to provide accurate analysis, but to create a sense of inevitability around his conclusions. His writing is filled with historical metaphors, many of which are selective, misleading, or outright ahistorical.

The Progressive Cathedral as a Secular Church

One of Yarvin's most influential rhetorical creations is **the Cathedral**, his term for the combined influence of academia, media, and bureaucracy. He argues that progressivism functions like a religion, where universities act as theological seminaries, journalists serve as the clergy, and dissenters are punished for heresy.

This metaphor is powerful because it allows him to:

- **Claim that progressivism is irrational and dogmatic**, placing it on the same level as religious fundamentalism.

- **Position himself as a rebellious truth-teller**, fighting against an entrenched ideological system.
- **Imply that democracy is an illusion** - since real power supposedly lies with unelected bureaucratic institutions rather than elected officials.

However, the **Cathedral framework is intentionally vague**. Yarvin never provides clear evidence that universities, media, and bureaucrats are coordinating in a unified way. Instead, he relies on implication and suggestion, allowing his followers to fill in the gaps with their own suspicions and grievances.

The "History Moves in Cycles" Argument

Another of Yarvin's favorite rhetorical techniques is presenting history as an **inevitable cycle of rise and decay**, where democracy is just a temporary phase before a return to "stable" hierarchical rule.

By invoking this **cyclical view of history**, he implies that resisting neoreaction is futile - eventually, all societies must return to rule by elites. However, this is **not a serious historical argument** so much as a justification for authoritarianism disguised as inevitability. The reality is that history is shaped by **contingent events, economic developments, and social movements**, not deterministic cycles.

Strategic Ambiguity: The Art of Saying Without Saying

Yarvin's writing is filled with **hints, suggestions, and provocations that never quite become direct statements**. He often presents controversial claims with a layer of plausible deniability, allowing him to backtrack if challenged.

For example:

- Instead of saying, “women should not have the right to vote,” he muses about whether women’s suffrage has led to poor governance and frames it as a “thought experiment.”
- Instead of explicitly endorsing racial hierarchies, he brings up “human biodiversity” and lets his audience draw the conclusions.
- Instead of calling for dictatorship outright, he suggests that democracy is unworkable and then *lets the reader wonder* what the logical alternative is.

This **strategic vagueness** serves multiple purposes:

1. **It makes his ideas sound less extreme** - by presenting them as open-ended questions rather than direct calls to action.
2. **It allows him to attract a broader audience** - those who may be curious about reactionary politics but not yet fully radicalized.
3. **It provides cover when confronted** - he can always claim he was just “exploring possibilities” rather than making prescriptive claims.

Audience Segmentation: Tailoring the Message

Yarvin carefully adjusts his tone and language depending on his audience. This segmentation allows him to appeal to different groups without alienating others.

- **For mainstream tech audiences:** He presents himself as a *governance futurist*, discussing “state

optimization" and "patching democracy" in ways that sound non-threatening.
- **For reactionary circles:** He drops the euphemisms and leans into the idea that democracy must be dismantled.
- **For the intellectually curious but skeptical reader:** He couches his claims in **pseudo-academic detachment**, making them sound exploratory rather than prescriptive.

This multi-layered messaging allows him to **pull people deeper into his worldview over time**. Readers who start out engaging with his mild critiques of democracy often find themselves, months later, reconsidering whether monarchy might actually be a good idea.

THE SLOW RADICALIZATION OF THE READER

Yarvin's writing is designed to move readers **step by step** toward more extreme conclusions. His rhetorical progression typically follows this pattern:

1. **"Democracy has flaws."** (mild skepticism)
2. **"Democracy is inefficient."** (neutral-sounding critique)
3. **"Democracy is a deception controlled by elites."** (conspiratorial framing)
4. **"Maybe governance should be hierarchical."** (hinting at authoritarianism)
5. **"Maybe democracy should be abandoned entirely."** (fully reactionary conclusion)

This gradual process makes his worldview seem more

reasonable and logical at each step, preventing readers from immediately rejecting his ideas as too extreme.

Conclusion: Understanding Yarvin's Persuasion Tactics

Yarvin's success lies not in his political insights but in his **ability to package old reactionary ideas in new, persuasive ways**. By rebranding monarchy as "corporate governance," using selective historical metaphors, and relying on strategic ambiguity, he has been able to push deeply anti-democratic ideas into mainstream tech and political discourse.

Understanding these rhetorical strategies is key to **deconstructing their influence** - not just in Yarvin's writing, but in the broader reactionary movement. His ideas thrive **not because they are correct, but because they are cleverly marketed**.

The Cathedral and the Hidden Power Structure

What is the Cathedral?

Yarvin presents democracy as an illusion, claiming that real power is held not by elected politicians but by an **elite class of academics, journalists, and bureaucrats** - what he calls *The Cathedral*. This is one of his most influential rhetorical constructs, framing progressive institutions as an all-encompassing, conspiratorial force. However, the Cathedral is **an intentionally vague and overstated concept** - Yarvin never provides direct evidence that universities, media, and bureaucrats operate as a single coordinated entity.

By framing progressivism as a "state religion," Yarvin tries to paint any institutional consensus as ideological enforcement, ignoring the fact that disagreements within academia and media are frequent and visible. His model also **conveniently ignores conservative power structures**, such as right-wing media, corporate lobbying, and think tanks, which exert just as much influence on public discourse but do not fit into his framework.

WHAT MAKES THE CATHEDRAL SO POWERFUL?

Yarvin believes the Cathedral is self-replicating. Unlike an authoritarian government that controls speech through censorship laws, **the Cathedral enforces ideological conformity through cultural and professional pressure.**

It does not imprison dissenters. Instead, it marginalizes them, ensuring that their ideas remain outside of mainstream discourse. This is why Yarvin describes the Cathedral as more insidious than an overt dictatorship - it maintains power while pretending to be neutral.

For example, if someone questions "progressive ideology" in academia or media, they are not formally punished, but they may lose career opportunities, be socially ostracized, or be labeled as extremists. Over time, this prevents alternative viewpoints from gaining legitimacy. According to Yarvin, this process explains why **major institutions - from Ivy League universities to corporate HR departments - seem to converge on the same progressive worldview** despite no central authority dictating their policies.

WHERE DID THE CATHEDRAL COME FROM?

Yarvin traces the Cathedral's origins back to Protestant New England. In his view, **modern progressivism is simply a secular evolution of Puritan moralism.**

He contends that elite universities like Harvard and Yale, originally founded as religious institutions, shifted over time from promoting Christian theology to promoting a new moral framework based on equality, democracy, and social justice. These universities, in turn, trained the bureaucrats, journalists, and policymakers who now run Western institutions. Yarvin believes that **even though modern progressivism claims to be secular, it functions like a religious**

doctrine, enforcing a moral order just as rigidly as Puritan New England once did.

Does This Mean Democracy is Fake?

Yarvin's argument is that democratic elections do not change the deeper ideological system. Even if voters elect a conservative government, the institutions shaping policy and public opinion remain the same.

To Yarvin, these patterns reveal that democracy is a ritual, not a true transfer of power: right-wing politicians who "moderate" their views once in office, the media's ability to delegitimize elected leaders (by labeling them threats to democracy), and the administrative state blocking reforms through bureaucracy and legal challenges.

To Yarvin, these patterns reveal that **democracy is a ritual, not a true transfer of power**. The real rulers are the unelected elites who set the ideological boundaries of acceptable governance.

Questions to Consider

- Is Yarvin right that institutions reinforce a single ideological framework, or does he overstate their coordination?
- Are elections meaningless if institutional power remains unchanged, or do elected officials still have real influence?
- Does modern progressivism function like a religion, as Yarvin suggests, or is it simply an evolving political ideology?

Testing the Framework

Yarvin's theory of the Cathedral is compelling but flawed in key ways.

First, **it assumes too much ideological unity among elites.** Universities, media organizations, and bureaucracies do not always agree - they contain internal debates, factions, and even rivalries.

Second, **his theory does not explain why ideological shifts happen**. If the Cathedral was as rigid as he claims, how did past social changes - such as the rise of neoliberal economics in the 1980s or the decline of mainstream religious influence - occur?

Finally, **Yarvin downplays the role of conservative institutions** in shaping power. Right-wing think tanks, corporate lobbying, and religious organizations have significant influence, yet they do not fit neatly into his Cathedral framework.

Key Takeaways

The Cathedral, in Yarvin's view, is the true power structure in modern society - a network of academic, media, and bureaucratic institutions that shape public opinion and policy.

This system enforces ideological conformity through social and professional pressure, rather than through direct government control.

Democracy becomes largely ceremonial in this framework, as elected governments must operate within the Cathedral's ideological boundaries.

However, **his argument oversimplifies "elite" institutions** - real power structures are more fragmented and contested than he suggests.

CONNECT THE DOTS

First, consider the big questions:

- How much do institutions really coordinate and enforce a single ideology?
- What real power do elected officials have within Yarvin's framework?
- Does progressivism actually function like a religion, as he claims? How so and to what extent?

Now, pick three major social changes from the past 50 years. For each, map out:

1. The key supporters and opponents
2. Which institutions drove or resisted change
3. Evidence for or against institutional coordination
4. Alternative explanations beyond the Cathedral theory

Some examples to consider: same-sex marriage legalization, 1980s free-market economics, marijuana policy shifts, immigration reform, or environmental regulations.

As you analyze these cases, ask:

1. What does the Cathedral framework explain well?
2. Where does this explanation fall short?
3. What competing theories might work better?

LOOKING AHEAD

For the next chapter on democracy, keep these questions in mind:

- How do anti-establishment movements succeed if the Cathedral is so powerful?
- What distinguishes institutional consensus from conspiracy?
- When is institutional agreement based on evidence versus conformity?

The Failure of Democracy

Why Does Yarvin Think Democracy is a Mistake?

Yarvin casts democracy as **not merely flawed, but inherently doomed**- a system that will always lead to corruption, inefficiency, and decline. His critique hinges on three core claims: that politicians prioritize re-election over long-term governance, that voters are too irrational to make informed decisions, and that entrenched bureaucratic elites ultimately hold real power. However, **each of these claims is built on selective evidence and ignores counterexamples.**

For instance, while **short-term political incentives exist, many democratic nations have developed mechanisms to counterbalance them**- such as independent central banks, long-term infrastructure planning, and judicial review. Meanwhile, Yarvin's claim that bureaucrats hold more power than elected officials is **contradicted by frequent shifts in policy when governments change hands,** as seen in major legislative reversals like Brexit or U.S. healthcare laws.

Unlike many critics of democracy, **Yarvin does not believe the system simply needs reform**. He argues that the very structure of democracy makes it unworkable and that no amount of tinkering can fix its fundamental flaws.

Does Democracy Actually Work?

One of Yarvin's core claims is that democracy does not select for competence. He argues that successful organizations - businesses, militaries, and even **well-run monarchies - operate under hierarchical decision-making**. In contrast, democracies rely on mass voting, which he sees as a recipe for failure.

He views democratic politics as a **popularity contest,** rewarding those who can campaign effectively rather than those who can govern well. **Politicians must appeal to the emotions** of the electorate, making promises that often contradict economic and strategic realities.

For example, Yarvin argues that elected leaders prioritize public approval over good governance, leading to excessive welfare spending, short-term economic fixes, and reactionary policymaking. He sees voter ignorance as a structural issue - most people lack the expertise to make informed decisions about governance, yet they still vote on complex issues. Moreover, democratic states are internally unstable because they rely on constantly shifting coalitions and public opinion, rather than a stable leadership structure.

The Illusion of Choice

According to Yarvin, democracy is not just inefficient - it is fundamentally deceptive. He believes that elections give the public **the illusion of control**, while real power remains in the hands of bureaucrats, media elites, and institutional administrators.

In his view, **democratic* politicians do not actually govern.** Instead, they operate within an entrenched system where major decisions are made by unelected officials, civil servants, and international institutions. Even when a new leader is elected, they must conform to pre-existing institutional norms.

Yarvin points to several patterns: presidents who fail to enact major reforms despite campaign promises, government agencies and courts that override elected officials through bureaucratic resistance and judicial rulings, and the media's ability to control public perception, shaping which policies are politically viable. To Yarvin, this means that **democracy is not actually a system of self-rule - it is an elaborate façade designed to maintain elite control** while making people believe they have a say in governance.

If Democracy is Bad, What's the Alternative?

Yarvin's alternative to democracy is a system of centralized rule based on "competence." Instead of elections, governance should be structured more like a well-run corporation, where decision-making is left to those with the expertise and long-term incentives to rule effectively.

His proposed alternative - **Neocameralism** - will be covered in depth in the next chapter, but the basic premise is that governments should be run like businesses, with a

---

* When we talk about 'democracy' throughout this book, we're referring to democratic systems and principles in general (small-d 'democratic'), not specifically the Democratic Party in the United States (big-D 'Democratic'). This distinction matters because Yarvin's critique targets democratic governance as a whole, not any particular political party.

sovereign CEO or ruler who acts as a long-term steward. Voters would be replaced by stakeholders, such as property owners, experts, or a governing elite. Bureaucracies would be structured like corporate departments, accountable only to the sovereign rather than to public opinion. Yarvin sees this as a system that prioritizes stability and efficiency over popularity.

Testing the Framework

Yarvin's critique of democracy raises valid points - politicians often make bad decisions to please voters, and bureaucracies do hold significant power. However, his argument has several significant weaknesses.

1. **He ignores successful democracies.** His theory assumes that all democratic systems fail, yet many have produced long-term stability and economic growth. The United States, despite its flaws, has remained intact for over two centuries. Nations like Switzerland, Japan, and Germany have maintained democratic governance alongside economic prosperity and political stability.
2. **He overlooks the failures of non-democratic regimes**. Yarvin idealizes monarchy and corporate governance, but many authoritarian states have collapsed due to corruption, power struggles, and mismanagement. His preferred system of "competent rule" has often produced catastrophic failures, from absolute monarchies plagued by succession crises to 20th-century dictatorships that ended in ruin. From the USSR to Zimbabwe, from Chile to the Third Reich - history offers far more examples of authoritarian failure than success.

3. **He contradicts himself on elite control**. On one hand, he argues that democracy is fake because real power lies with bureaucrats and elites. Yet he also claims that governance should be handed over to elites who would rule directly. If elites already dominate the system, why would giving them absolute power make things better?

CONNECT THE DOTS

Consider a major policy decision in your country's recent history. Analyze it through Yarvin's framework:

Follow the decision-making process:

- What was promised during campaigns?
- What actually happened once in office?
- Who really made the key decisions?

Look for evidence of:

- Short-term thinking vs. long-term planning
- Voter influence vs. institutional control
- Public opinion vs. bureaucratic power

Then ask yourself:

- Did this decision demonstrate democracy's weaknesses or strengths?
- Would a non-democratic system have handled it better?
- What alternative decision-making process might have worked?

Looking Ahead

As we move into the next chapter on Neocameralism, consider:

- Can corporate governance really work for entire societies?
- How would succession work in Yarvin's system?
- What happens when competent rule becomes incompetent?

Neocameralism

What is Neocameralism?

Yarvin's alternative to democracy is *Neocameralism*- a system that **masks autocracy under the language of corporate governance.** Instead of elected leadership, the state is run as a business, with a **"sovereign CEO"** replacing politicians and elections. He claims this model would be **more efficient, long-term-oriented, and immune to democratic dysfunction**- but this framing is misleading.

By **replacing the language of monarchy with corporate jargon,** Yarvin attempts to make autocracy sound modern and practical rather than regressive. But in reality, **corporate governance does not automatically ensure good leadership**- companies frequently suffer from corruption, self-serving executives, and catastrophic failures (e.g., Enron, WeWork, and FTX). His vision assumes a benevolent CEO-ruler, **ignoring how unchecked corporate power often leads to short-term profit-seeking at the expense of the public good.**

This raises troubling questions about the nature of citizenship and human rights. In Yarvin's system, **citizens effectively become assets** to be managed rather than participants in governance. Their value to the state would be measured primarily in economic terms - their productivity, their consumption, their contribution to state wealth. **Those unable to contribute economically might be seen as liabilities** rather than citizens deserving of protection and support.

While Yarvin argues this would lead to better governance (since the ruler would want to maintain valuable "human capital"), history suggests a darker outcome. When people are treated as state property, the result tends toward exploitation rather than protection. Whether in serfdom or slavedom or company towns of the Industrial Revolution or modern authoritarian capitalism, systems that prioritize state/corporate wealth over citizen welfare typically create something closer to bondage than efficient governance.

The fundamental problem is that Yarvin's model **reduces complex human societies to pure economic units.** Many would argue, counter to Yarvin, that a nation exists for more than wealth accumulation - it's a community with social bonds, cultural heritage, and moral obligations to its members. By treating the state as merely a profit-generating enterprise, Neocameralism ignores these crucial human elements of governance.

Yarvin believes democracy's fundamental flaw is that it selects leaders based on their ability to win votes rather than their competence in governance. Under his system, political power is not distributed among voters but consolidated in the hands of a sovereign executive who is accountable only to the state's shareholders.

HOW WOULD A NEOCAMERALIST GOVERNMENT WORK?

Yarvin envisions a fully privatized government, where the state is owned and managed like a commercial enterprise. The system works like this:

1. The state functions as a company, with the ruler as CEO and influential stakeholders as shareholders.
2. **Citizens do not vote or participate in policymaking.** Instead, those who "own shares" in the government have influence proportional to their ownership, just as stockholders do in a corporation.*
3. **Laws are** not written by legislators but are **determined by what best serves the interests of the government's owners. Security forces operate as a private enforcement arm** rather than as institutions subject to political oversight. There are no political parties, no independent media challenging the regime, and no competing branches of government.
4. If the country functions well, its value increases, benefiting the sovereign and shareholders. If it fails, the ruler risks losing control - though Yarvin is notably vague about exactly how this would work.

---

* Some may say this theory is echoed in JD Vance's proposed voting system wherein parents would receive additional votes based on their number of children, effectively disenfranchising citizens without children. This mirrors Curtis Yarvin's "neocameralist" model where political influence is distributed like corporate shares, with "stakeholders" having power proportional to their ownership rather than through universal citizenship-based voting.

Why Does Yarvin Prefer CEOs to Presidents or Prime Ministers?

To Yarvin, the difference between a democratic leader and a corporate CEO is simple: **a president is incentivized to think short-term (winning elections), while a CEO must optimize for long-term value.**

He argues that corporations operate under clearer, more effective decision-making structures. A CEO is appointed based on competence, not popularity. They can focus on what works rather than what sells to voters. Companies must be profitable to survive, meaning they are disciplined by market forces rather than public opinion.

In Yarvin's view, if states functioned more like businesses, they would be governed with the same efficiency and pragmatism that successful companies display. The ruler would have no reason to pander to special interests or manipulate public sentiment, as they would hold absolute control and be judged solely on results.

Isn't This Just Monarchy With a New Name?

Neocameralism is essentially monarchy rebranded for the tech age. While Yarvin initially presented himself as an advocate of monarchy, he later shifted to using corporate governance as his model. The structure remains the same - rule by a single, unchallenged leader - but the language has changed.

This shift in rhetoric is strategic. While monarchy sounds archaic, corporate governance suggests modernity and efficiency. By presenting absolute rule in business terms, Yarvin makes his ideas more palatable to libertarians and tech entrepreneurs who already see democracy as inefficient.

The sovereign CEO of a Neocameralist state would function exactly like a monarch, but with ownership rights rather than divine right as the source of authority. It's a repackaging exercise, not a fundamental change in political theory.

Testing the Framework

Despite Yarvin's promises of rational, efficient governance, Neocameralism faces several fundamental challenges.

1. **Governments and businesses serve fundamentally different purposes.** A corporation exists to maximize profit, while a government must provide justice, ensure rights, maintain social stability, and protect its citizens. If a state functions purely as an enterprise, it might **treat its population as resources to be exploited** rather than citizens to be served.
2. **Corporate governance is not immune to the problems Yarvin identifies in democracy.** Business executives can engage in self-dealing, short-term thinking, and value-destroying behavior. Many corporations have been ruined by leaders who prioritized quick profits over long-term sustainability. Without democratic checks and balances, what would prevent a "sovereign CEO" from doing the same?
3. **Neocameralism lacks a viable mechanism for leadership change.** In a democracy, elections provide regular opportunities to remove bad leaders. Under Yarvin's system, **an incompetent or corrupt ruler could maintain power indefinitely.** He never adequately explains how shareholders could remove a failing CEO-monarch who refuses to step down.

4. **Historical examples undermine Yarvin's case.** Both monarchies and corporations have frequently collapsed due to mismanagement, infighting, and corruption - the very problems he claims Neocameralism would solve. His assumption that concentrated power leads to better governance ignores centuries of evidence to the contrary.

Connect the Dots

Consider a major corporation you know well. Now imagine it running your entire country:

Map out the practical implications:

- How would public services work?
- What would happen to those who can't pay?
- How would rights be protected?

Follow the incentives:

- Would maximizing state value align with public good?
- How would the rulers balance profit against other goals?
- What would prevent exploitation of citizens?

Examine historical parallels:

- What examples exist of corporate-style governance?
- How did they handle these challenges?
- What lessons do they offer?

Looking Ahead

As we explore the implications of Neocameralism, consider:

- How would citizenship work in a corporate state?
- What happens to those who can't afford to "exit"?
- Can any single ruler, however competent, effectively govern a complex modern society?

A New Feudalism: Neocameral Society

Yarvin argues that **most people are naturally suited to being "managed" rather than participating in governance.** He believes that hierarchy is natural and that most people would be better off accepting their **role as productive "assets"** of the state rather than trying to participate in governance.

His view is essentially that:

- Most **people lack the capacity** for meaningful participation in governance
- They would be **better off being "well-managed"** by competent **elites**
- Their **value is primarily measured in economic terms**
- Social welfare should exist only to the extent it maintains productive capacity
- **Rights exist only as property rights,** not as inherent human rights

So while he presents Neocameralism in terms of efficiency and stability, it fundamentally reduces human beings to economic units whose only purpose is to generate value for the sovereign and shareholders. It's effectively a form of neo-feudalism dressed up in corporate language. Instead of kings and nobles, we have CEOs and shareholders. Instead of serfs, we have "customers."

Yarvin's Social Vision

In Neocameralism, society is explicitly divided into distinct classes with no pretense of equality.

1. At the top sit the sovereign and shareholders who own the state.
2. Below them, a professional class manages day-to-day operations.
3. At the bottom - the vast majority of people - are "customers" who exist primarily to generate value for the owners.

This isn't just a political theory - it's a **complete reimagining of human society.**

- Rights would be based on property ownership rather than citizenship.
- Welfare would exist only when profitable for the state.
- Education would focus on producing productive workers rather than engaged citizens.
- Democracy and political participation would be replaced by "consumer choice" - the theoretical ability to leave if you're unhappy.

Historical Parallels

To understand what this system would actually look like, we can examine similar experiments throughout history.

British Rule in Ireland provides a stark example of Yarvin's governance principles in practice. The British system wasn't just about remote control - it embodied core beliefs that mirror Neocameralism: that most people lack capacity for self-governance, that they're better off under "competent" elite management, and that human value is primarily economic.

During the Great Famine, this ideology justified continuing food exports while over a million Irish died or fled - property rights trumped human rights, and Irish suffering was seen as proof of their unfitness to rule themselves rather than a result of the system. The British government's actions and inactions were based on their ideological view of the Irish as inferior and their belief that population reduction might actually benefit Ireland. Any resistance was treated as confirmation that the Irish needed firm governance rather than evidence of the system's failure. This genocide reveals how theories of "natural" ruling classes tend to create self-reinforcing cycles of repression and resistance.

Apartheid South Africa exemplifies how Yarvin's vision of formalized, tiered citizenship inevitably requires systematic violence and repression. The apartheid system went beyond just restricting voting rights - it created an elaborate legal framework that, like Neocameralism, treated governance as a technical problem to be solved through "rational" management of different population groups. The National Party justified this through similar logic: that only certain groups were capable of self-governance, that others needed to be "developed" separately under supervision, and that resistance proved the need for stronger controls rather than systemic change.

The system claimed to be about "separate development," but in practice created a highly efficient mechanism for extracting labor while minimizing obligations to the laborers - much like Yarvin's emphasis on treating citizens as human capital rather than rights-bearing individuals.

Despite (or because of) its elaborate theoretical justifications and legal frameworks, the system required increasingly costly repression to maintain, faced growing internal resistance and international isolation, and ultimately collapsed - demonstrating how governance systems based on explicit hierarchy and restricted rights generate their own opposition regardless of how thoroughly they're rationalized.

Company Towns offer perhaps the clearest parallel. In places like Pullman, Illinois, one corporation owned everything - housing, stores, schools, and jobs. While presented as benevolent paternalism, these **experiments typically led to exploitation.** When profits fell, so did wages and services. When workers protested, they faced eviction from company-owned housing. The ultimate failure of company towns - often ending in violent labor disputes - reveals the inherent instability of corporate governance over human communities.

Modern Corporate States like Singapore and Dubai are frequently cited by Yarvin, but his analysis is selective. While he praises Singapore's efficiency, he ignores its extensive public housing and healthcare systems. He admires Dubai's business-friendly policies but overlooks its dependence on migrant labor with few rights. These states manage to function precisely because they provide more public services and protections than Yarvin's model would allow.

. . .

Historical Feudalism provides another crucial reference point. Medieval European manors and Japanese daimyo domains operated on similar principles to Neocameralism - absolute rulers, hierarchical society, and subjects valued primarily for their productive capacity. These systems consistently faced problems Yarvin doesn't adequately address: succession crises, noble infighting, peasant revolts, and eventual collapse.

Life Under Neocameralism

What would this mean for different social classes?

- **The Shareholders would form a new nobility, owning not just companies but sovereign rights over territory and population.** Their power would be checked only by other shareholders, creating the same kind of instability that plagued feudal aristocracies.
- **The Professional Class would serve as modern vassals** - trained technicians, managers, and administrators dependent on shareholder approval. While materially comfortable, they would lack true autonomy, their position always contingent on loyalty to the owners.
- **The General Population would effectively become modern serfs.** Without political rights or guaranteed protections, their value to the state would be purely economic. Social services would exist only to maintain productive capacity. Education would focus on job skills rather than critical thinking. Those unable to generate

sufficient value would be seen as liabilities rather than citizens deserving support.

TESTING THE FRAMEWORK

Yarvin's model faces several fundamental problems:

1. It assumes perfect alignment between profit and public good. History shows this is rarely true - profitable decisions often harm public welfare, from environmental destruction to worker exploitation.
2. It lacks mechanisms for preventing abuse. Without democratic checks or legal rights, what stops rulers from exploiting their population? Yarvin's answer - that damaging your human capital is bad business - ignores countless historical examples of profitable exploitation.
3. It ignores human dignity and aspirations. People are not merely economic units to be managed. Systems that treat them as such typically face resistance, instability, and eventual collapse.
4. It overlooks the complexity of modern society. Contemporary nations require more than just efficient management - they need innovation, creativity, and engaged citizens. Reducing everyone to servants of state profit would likely decrease rather than increase national success.

The historical record consistently contradicts Yarvin's assumptions:

- Company towns collapsed under their own contradictions.

- Feudal systems proved unstable and inefficient.
- Authoritarian capitalism often produces corruption and stagnation.
- The most successful modern societies tend to combine market efficiency with strong democratic institutions and civil rights.

Connect the Dots

Consider your own position in this system.

Where would you fit in the hierarchy?

- What rights would you have?
- How would you advance?
- What would happen if you fell ill or lost your job?

Examine historical examples:

- Why did company towns fail?
- What happened to societies with similar structures?
- What lessons do these examples offer?

Follow the incentives:

- Who benefits from this system?
- What prevents abuse of power?
- How would innovation and progress occur?

Looking Ahead

As we continue examining Yarvin's ideas, keep in mind what they would mean in practice. While he presents Neocameralism as a modern, efficient system, its social structure closely resembles forms of governance that historically led to exploitation, stagnation, and collapse.

The question isn't just whether such a system could work, but whether it represents a society in which most people would want to live.

Religion in the Neocameral State

Yarvin's treatment of religion reveals core contradictions in neocameralist thought. While many of his modern followers advocate for Christian nationalism, Yarvin himself views **religion primarily as a tool for social control** - more akin to corporate culture management than divine truth. This tension between instrumental and theological approaches to religion exposes broader questions about authority, legitimacy, and social control in the neocameral state.

The **instrumental approach** sees religion as a tool or technology for social control and cohesion:

- Religion exists to maintain order and stability
- Religious beliefs can be engineered and managed
- Truth claims are secondary to social utility
- Religious practices are evaluated by their effectiveness at producing desired behaviors
- Similar to how corporations manage company culture

The **theological approach** sees religion as a source of absolute truth and divine authority:

- Religious doctrine comes from divine revelation
- Truth claims are primary and non-negotiable
- Religious obligations override worldly concerns
- Religious authority derives from God, not human institutions
- Cannot be modified for convenience or profit

The key tension is that **Yarvin's theory requires the instrumental approach (treating religion as a manageable asset)** while many of his followers take the theological approach (believing in absolute religious truth). These views fundamentally conflict - one can't simultaneously believe Christianity is divine truth AND treat it as an adjustable tool for social control.

WHAT ROLE DOES RELIGION PLAY?

Yarvin's writings on religion are strikingly corporate in their outlook. He treats **faith as a "social technology" for maintaining order and cohesion,** explicitly rejecting claims of absolute religious truth in favor of pragmatic utility. This mirrors earlier absolutist thinkers like Hobbes, who saw religion primarily as a tool of state control.

For Yarvin, the existence of some form of **"state religion" is inevitable - but its specific content is arbitrary.** What matters is its effectiveness at producing desired social outcomes, not its theological validity. This instrumentalist approach treats **religious belief as something to be engineered** and managed rather than something that emerges organically or contains inherent truth.

The Christian Nationalist Paradox

Many of Yarvin's contemporary followers embrace Christian nationalism while advocating for neocameralist governance. This creates an immediate contradiction: how can divine law coexist with shareholder supremacy? Christian nationalism posits absolute moral truths and divine authority, while neocameralism reduces all decisions to property rights and efficiency.

A truly corporate state would have to treat **Christianity as just another asset to be managed - potentially to be modified or discarded if it impacted profitability.** This fundamental tension is rarely addressed by those attempting to merge these ideologies.

Historical Precedents and Problems

Previous **attempts to reconcile religious authority with absolute state control offer cautionary tales.** The Soviet Union's attempt to replace religion with state ideology produced decades of underground resistance. Singapore's attempt to manage multiple religions through bureaucratic control remains tenuous. Even the Tudor monarchy's creation of a state church led to centuries of religious conflict. These examples suggest that treating religion as a mere tool of governance inevitably produces resistance from true believers.

The Corporate-Religious Conflict

Real-world examples of corporate religious management reveal practical problems for neocameralism. Company towns often built churches and supported religious activities, but conflicts emerged when religious obligations conflicted with profit motives. Modern corporations face similar challenges managing religious accommodation. These tensions would be dramatically amplified in a neocameral state, where corporate authority claims total sovereignty.

Basic questions remain unresolved:

- Would religious law override shareholder interests?
- How would competing religious claims be managed?
- Could religious obligations limit profit-seeking activities?
- Who would have authority over religious doctrine?

Testing the Framework

Yarvin's instrumentalist approach to religion faces several key challenges:

1. It assumes religious belief can be managed like corporate culture. History shows that true religious conviction often resists attempts at bureaucratic control, producing underground movements and sustained resistance.
2. His theory doesn't account for competing religious claims. While company towns could impose a single denomination, modern states must manage multiple faiths. Singapore's example shows how this requires constant state intervention and surveillance.
3. The fundamental conflict between profit motives and religious obligations remains unresolved. When company towns faced this conflict, business interests invariably won - but this generated ongoing tension and resistance.

Connect the Dots

First, consider these fundamental questions:

- Can religious belief really be managed like corporate culture?
- What happens when profit motives conflict with religious obligations?
- How do states maintain legitimacy without genuine religious authority?
- Is there a difference between engineered and organic religious conviction?

Now, pick three historical examples of state management of religion. For each, analyze:

- How the state attempted to control religious practice
- What resistance emerged and why
- Whether certain approaches proved more stable than others
- How conflicts between state and religious authority were resolved

Some examples to consider:

- Tudor England's creation of the Anglican Church
- Singapore's bureaucratic management of multiple faiths
- Ottoman Empire's millet system
- Japanese State Shinto
- American civil religion and "In God We Trust"
- Soviet state atheism and underground churches

As you analyze these cases, ask:

- What methods of religious control proved most effective?
- Where did resistance emerge and why?
- How did economic interests interact with religious authority?
- What alternative approaches might work better?

LOOKING AHEAD

For the next chapter on sovereignty and legitimacy, keep these questions in mind:

- How do corporate states maintain legitimacy without traditional religious authority?
- Can engineered belief systems replace organic religious conviction?
- What happens when shareholders and believers clash?
- Is some form of state religion inevitable, as Yarvin claims?
- How do religious institutions resist or adapt to state control?
- What role does genuine belief play in social stability?

The Case for Restricting the Vote

Yarvin does not believe in universal suffrage. He argues that allowing everyone to vote leads to poor governance because most people are uninformed, irrational, and easily manipulated. In his view, democracy functions as an illusion of power, where the masses believe they are governing themselves when in reality, the system is controlled by entrenched elites. Instead of broad participation, Yarvin proposes that **voting should be restricted to those who are, in his mind, "competent" to rule.**

His arguments against universal suffrage are neither new nor particularly sophisticated - they are a rehash of old aristocratic justifications for limiting political power to the elite. He claims that broad voting rights lead to irrational, emotional governance, arguing that **only the "competent" should participate in elections.** But his criteria for competence - whether property ownership, IQ, or financial stake - **are historically linked to exclusionary and often racist policies.**

His reasoning **echoes past justifications for restricting suffrage**, from early U.S. property requirements to Jim Crow literacy tests. More importantly, **it ignores how democratic participation has historically been correlated with increased political stability and economic growth.** Yarvin presents restricted suffrage as a form of governance optimization, but in practice, such systems have tended to concentrate power in the hands of self-serving elites rather than producing better outcomes.

Why Restrict Voting?

According to Yarvin, universal suffrage undermines effective governance in several ways:

1. The majority of voters lack the knowledge to make complex political decisions
2. People vote based on emotion rather than reason
3. Short-term thinking dominates over long-term strategy
4. Voters can be easily manipulated by media and rhetoric
5. Those without "skin in the game" make decisions affecting others

Who Should Be Allowed to Vote?

One approach is to limit voting to **property owners or taxpayers**, similar to early American democracy. Another possibility is an **IQ-based system**, where voting is restricted to those who pass a test of intelligence or political knowledge. A more extreme version of his argument is that **only an elite ruling class should have political power,** with no voting at all. In this model, governance is left to a group of competent leaders - whether appointed, hereditary, or self-selecting - who rule based on merit rather than popular will. This aligns with his broader preference for neocameralism, where a sovereign executive, rather than voters, determines the direction of the state.

Models of Restricted Suffrage

Yarvin does not offer a single, fixed alternative to universal suffrage. Instead, he presents **several possible models** for restricting the vote:

- **Property-Based:** Similar to early American democracy, this would restrict voting to property owners or taxpayers. The idea is that those who contribute financially to the system have a vested interest in making "responsible" political decisions.
- **Intelligence-Based:** Voting would be limited to those who pass tests of intelligence or political knowledge. This assumes that only those who can understand complex governance issues should participate in decision-making. Yarvin often suggests that modern democracy is flawed because it allows decisions to be made by an "uninformed" electorate, and that only those with the "intellectual capacity" to understand complex governance issues should participate.
- **Elite Rule:** The most extreme version eliminates voting entirely, leaving **governance to a "competent" ruling class** - whether appointed, hereditary, or self-selecting. This aligns with his broader preference for neocameralism.

The Property Requirement Problem

The idea that property ownership creates better voters contains several flawed assumptions:

1. Wealth doesn't equate to governance competence. History shows property-owning classes often make decisions based on narrow self-interest rather than public good. The Irish Famine provides a stark example - property-owning landlords continued exporting food while their tenants starved, demonstrating how property qualifications can produce devastating governance failures.
2. Property requirements inherently privilege inheritance over merit. Most wealth historically comes from inheritance rather than individual achievement. This creates a self-perpetuating aristocracy based on birth rather than competence - precisely the kind of system that even Yarvin claims to oppose.
3. Property requirements ignore non-financial stakes in society. Teachers, nurses, military servicemembers, and many others make crucial contributions and have deep investment in good governance without necessarily owning significant property. The assumption that only property represents "skin in the game" fundamentally misunderstands what gives people a stake in society's success.

The Intelligence Testing Problem

The idea of restricting voting to those who can pass intelligence or knowledge tests presents several fundamental problems:

1. There's the question of who designs and administers these tests. Any system of testing would itself become a tool of power - those who control the tests effectively control access to political participation. History shows these systems are inevitably used to exclude disfavored groups while preserving the power of existing elites.
2. The assumption that intelligence or formal knowledge predicts good governance judgment is deeply flawed. Many of history's most catastrophic political decisions were made by highly educated elites. Raw intelligence or academic knowledge doesn't guarantee wisdom, ethical judgment, or understanding of ordinary people's needs.
3. Defining "political knowledge" is inherently subjective and political. What counts as valid political knowledge? Whose version of history or economics is correct? These aren't neutral technical questions but deeply contested political ones. Making them into requirements for voting rights simply moves political power from the ballot box to the test makers.
4. Intelligence and knowledge tests for voting rights have a dark history as tools of racial and class exclusion in the Jim Crow South and elsewhere. While Yarvin presents this as a technical solution for improving governance quality, in practice such systems have consistently served to maintain existing power structures while providing a veneer of objective legitimacy.

The Elite Rule Problem

The idea of restricting voting to a select elite class faces even more fundamental issues:

1. It assumes elites will prioritize good governance over self-interest. Historical aristocracies and oligarchies demonstrate the opposite - without accountability, ruling classes tend toward corruption, rent-seeking, and protecting their privileges rather than serving the broader public good.
2. Elite rule creates a dangerous disconnect between rulers and the ruled. Without meaningful input from the broader population, elite decision-makers become increasingly isolated from the real-world impacts of their choices. This typically produces both bad governance and growing social instability.
3. Elite systems lack mechanisms for peaceful change. When rulers are unaccountable to the public, the only real check on poor governance becomes violent resistance. This is why purely elite systems tend to end in revolution or collapse.
4. Elite rule faces a legitimacy problem. Modern societies generally reject the idea that any group has an inherent right to rule others. Without some form of popular consent, elite systems must rely increasingly on force and coercion to maintain power - creating exactly the kind of instability Yarvin claims to want to avoid.

The Women's Suffrage Question

One of Yarvin's more extreme assertions is that **women's suffrage was a mistake.** He argues that granting women the right to vote has contributed to the decline of governance by making politics more sentimental, moralistic, and short-termist. He asserts that women as a bloc tend to **favor policies prioritizing welfare and social stability over efficiency and strategic thinking.**

Yarvin frames this as an objective assessment of voting patterns rather than a personal attack on women. He claims that **if politics is to be based on rational decision-making rather than emotional appeals, then it is necessary to reconsider whether universal suffrage** - including women's suffrage - was a wise political development.

This mirrors historical arguments against women's political participation, repackaged in the language of governance efficiency. It exemplifies how Yarvin often presents traditional reactionary positions through the lens of technical optimization rather than explicit value judgments.

This argument is not unique to Yarvin. Throughout history, reactionary thinkers have opposed women's political participation on the grounds that it disrupts traditional social hierarchies or weakens the state. Yarvin's version of the argument repackages this view in the language of governance efficiency, avoiding explicit moral claims while making the case that women's enfranchisement has made politics less effective.

Race and Restricted Suffrage

Yarvin's arguments about restricted voting rights cannot be separated from their racial implications. While he presents voting restrictions as neutral technical solutions for improving governance quality, historically such restrictions have consistently served as tools for racial exclusion and maintaining white political dominance.

The "property requirement" argument ignores how systematic racism has affected wealth accumulation and property ownership. His "intelligence testing" proposal echoes Jim Crow literacy tests that used seemingly objective criteria to systematically disenfranchise Black voters. Even his "elite rule" framework assumes a ruling class that has historically excluded racial minorities.

This reveals a broader pattern in Yarvin's work - repackaging historically racist policies in apparently neutral technical language. By focusing on abstract qualities like "competence" or "skin in the game" while ignoring the racial history of restricted suffrage, he obscures how these systems have consistently served to concentrate power in white hands.

Would Restricting the Vote Actually Improve Governance?

Yarvin presents suffrage restrictions as a way to improve governance by ensuring that only the most “capable” individuals have political power. However, his argument assumes that **elite rule automatically produces better outcomes.**

The idea that **property owners or the wealthy govern better** ignores the fact that many historical ruling classes have made catastrophic decisions based on self-interest rather than good governance. Aristocratic and oligarchic governments have often been corrupt, complacent, and more focused on preserving their own power than on serving the public good.

The **IQ-based voting model** also raises serious questions. Intelligence alone does not guarantee good judgment, and many high-IQ individuals hold wildly different political views. Furthermore, deciding who qualifies as intelligent enough to vote would introduce **a bureaucratic system that is itself open to manipulation and bias.**

The Hidden Contradiction in Yarvin's Argument

Yarvin's argument contains a fundamental tension: he claims democracy is already controlled by bureaucrats and unelected elites (the Cathedral) while simultaneously arguing for explicit elite rule. This raises a key question: if democracy is already an illusion masking elite control, how would formalizing elite power improve governance?

In essence, Yarvin is not proposing a radical alternative so much as **arguing for a system that already exists in practice,** only with different rulers. His model does not eliminate elite control - it merely replaces one group of elites with another, assuming that the new elite will be more competent.

Testing the Framework

Historical examples reveal several problems with restricted suffrage:

The Property Requirement: Early American democracy limited voting to property owners, but this system faced increasing resistance as it became clear that wealth didn't guarantee good judgment. Many property-owning elites made decisions based on narrow self-interest rather than public good.

Intelligence Tests: Jim Crow-era literacy tests demonstrated how seemingly objective requirements can be weaponized for discrimination. Even genuine intelligence tests raise questions - smart people often disagree radically about policy, and raw intelligence doesn't guarantee good governance.

Elite Rule: Historical aristocracies and oligarchies often became corrupt and complacent. Without accountability to the broader population, ruling classes tend to prioritize their own interests over effective governance.

Limiting voting rights also assumes that **ordinary citizens have no meaningful role in governance.** Even if some voters are uninformed, democratic participation ensures that political leaders remain accountable. Removing the right to vote from the majority of the population risks creating a system where rulers are completely detached from the people they govern, leading to resentment and instability.

Connect the Dots

Consider these questions:

- How have different societies determined who is "qualified" to vote?
- What happens when ruling classes become corrupt or incompetent?
- Can any system of restricted suffrage avoid becoming a tool for discrimination?
- How do we balance expertise with accountability?
- How can rulers be held accountable without universal suffrage?
- What determines legitimate authority if not popular consent?
- Can any system prevent elite capture while maintaining efficiency?
- How do different voting systems affect social stability?
- What role does perceived legitimacy play in governance?

Examine three historical cases of restricted voting rights. For each, analyze:

- The justification given for restrictions
- How the system actually functioned
- What resistance emerged and why
- How the system eventually changed or fell

Some examples to consider:

- Athenian citizenship requirements
- Medieval guild voting systems
- Jim Crow voting restrictions
- South African apartheid voting
- Historical property requirements
- Ancient Roman citizenship classes

Race, Ethnicity, and the Nation-State

Yarvin argues that **diverse societies are inherently unstable** and that political systems function best when they govern a population with a shared cultural, ethnic, or racial background. He claims that multiculturalism leads to social fragmentation, political dysfunction, and a breakdown of trust between citizens and the state. While he presents this as an objective assessment of historical trends, it raises fundamental questions about identity, governance, and social cohesion in his proposed system.

According to Yarvin, **historically successful civilizations were built on ethnic and cultural unity.** He argues that when a state governs people with vastly different traditions, values, and identities, it loses its ability to maintain order and legitimacy.

What Role Does Homogeneity Play?

According to Yarvin, historically successful civilizations were built on ethnic and cultural unity. His argument rests on several key claims:

- Social trust is higher in homogeneous societies because people feel a shared identity with their neighbors, which leads to better governance and stability.
- Diversity creates competing interest groups that weaken national unity, making it harder for the state to function effectively.
- Ethnic and cultural mixing leads to inevitable conflict, as different groups will always struggle for dominance.
- Different groups have inherent characteristics that affect governance capability.

He frames these arguments through pseudo-scientific rhetoric rather than explicit racial ideology, claiming to pursue optimal governance rather than ethnic supremacy. This mirrors his broader pattern of recasting traditional reactionary positions as technical problems to be solved. He believes that governance works best when it is aligned with a strong national identity based on race or culture.

Ethno-Nationalism

Yarvin does not explicitly call for an ethno-state, but he frequently argues that societies function best when they are **ruled by a dominant ethnic or cultural group.** He is skeptical of the idea that multiethnic states can be politically stable in the long run. While he does not advocate for forced segregation, his work asserts that a more homogeneous ruling class is preferable and that modern liberal democracies have eroded their own stability by embracing diversity. This distinction between advocating for an explicit ethno-state versus arguing for ethnic dominance and homogeneous rule is largely semantic - both positions ultimately justify racial hierarchy and exclusion.

He **suggests that mass migration has weakened Western societies** by introducing populations that do not share the same historical or cultural background. He frames immigration as a force that disrupts social cohesion, claiming that Western nations functioned better when they were culturally and racially more uniform.

Yarvin often refers to historical empires - such as the British Empire or the Austro-Hungarian Empire - to illustrate his point. He argues that these states only succeeded when their ruling class maintained **a strong internal identity**, despite governing diverse populations. When that identity weakened, the empire collapsed. He uses this to argue that **modern multicultural democracies are doomed to fail** because they lack a single, unifying identity.

These examples fail to accurately capture the collapse of these empires for several reasons:

Empire vs. Democracy is a False Comparison

Yarvin treats historical empires as analogous to modern multicultural democracies, but they are fundamentally different systems. The British and Austro-Hungarian Empires were *imperial* states that governed subject populations through coercion, economic extraction, and hierarchical control. Modern democracies, in contrast, attempt to integrate diverse populations through enfranchisement, shared institutions, and legal equality. The collapse of empires does not necessarily predict the failure of democracies, as their governance structures and internal dynamics are vastly different.

. . .

Empire Stability Did Not Depend Solely on Identity

Yarvin suggests that these empires collapsed because their ruling classes lost a unifying identity, but economic decline, military defeats, shifting global power structures, and nationalist movements played far greater roles. The Austro-Hungarian Empire disintegrated largely due to World War I, nationalist uprisings, and external pressures - not merely a loss of aristocratic cohesion. Similarly, the British Empire did not collapse due to internal identity crises but because of anti-colonial resistance, economic overextension, and changing global political realities.

Multiculturalism Was Integral to Empire

Contrary to Yarvin's framing, these empires functioned precisely *because* they adapted to multiethnic and multicultural realities. The British Empire ruled over vast, diverse populations by incorporating local elites into administrative structures and adapting governance to regional contexts. The Austro-Hungarian Empire, while plagued by nationalist tensions, survived for decades by balancing power among its various ethnic groups. The idea that these empires fell solely because they lacked a homogenous ruling identity ignores the complexity of how they actually operated.

Modern Democracies Function Differently from Empires

Yarvin's argument assumes that contemporary democracies require the same type of rigid ruling identity as imperial elites. However, modern democratic states rely on civic institutions, legal frameworks, and pluralistic governance rather than a singular ruling class. Countries like Canada, Switzerland, and the United States have successfully maintained national stability despite being multicultural, countering Yarvin's claim that diverse societies are inherently doomed.

In short, Yarvin misreads the historical record by reducing empire collapse to cultural identity loss while ignoring the geopolitical, economic, and military forces at play. His comparison between collapsing empires and contemporary multicultural democracies is fundamentally flawed, as it treats entirely different political models as if they were interchangeable.

The Human Biodiversity Question

Yarvin engages with "human biodiversity" (HBD), a fringe movement arguing that genetic differences between populations explain differences in intelligence, behavior, and governance capability. While avoiding explicit racial supremacy claims, he suggests biological differences determine political outcomes - ignoring how colonialism, economic systems, and historical inequalities shape societies. It is essentially neo-eugenics.

This mirrors historical "scientific racism," repackaged in modern technical language. Like earlier pseudo-scientific justifications for racial hierarchy, it selectively uses data while ignoring broader historical and social contexts.

What is Human Biodiversity (HBD) Theory?

Human Biodiversity (HBD) is a term used by certain political and ideological groups to describe the belief that genetic differences between human populations significantly influence intelligence, behavior, and social structures. Proponents argue that these genetic variations, often along racial or ethnic lines, explain disparities in economic success, crime rates, and political stability between different groups.

The term itself originates from discussions in evolutionary biology and population genetics but has been co-opted by race realists, white nationalists, and some reactionary thinkers - like Curtis Yarvin - to justify racial hierarchy, ethno-nationalism, or opposition to diversity policies. While mainstream genetics recognizes human variation, the way HBD is used in neoreactionary and far-right circles is widely considered pseudoscientific and politically motivated.

Origins of the HBD Concept

Early Eugenics and Racial Science (19th-20th Century)

Before the modern study of genetics, racial scientists in the 19th and early 20th centuries tried to classify human populations based on skull shape, skin color, and other physical features, often using these classifications to justify racial superiority theories.
Eugenics movements in the US and Europe promoted policies like forced sterilization and immigration restrictions under the assumption that certain populations were genetically inferior.

The Bell Curve (1994)

A major modern influence on HBD was *The Bell Curve* by Richard Herrnstein and Charles Murray, which argued that intelligence is largely hereditary and that racial IQ differences contribute to economic and social inequality.
The book was heavily criticized for its flawed methodology, reliance on dubious datasets, and failure to

account for socio-economic and environmental factors.

The Rise of Internet HBD Advocates (2000s-Present)

In the early 2000s, bloggers and forums helped popularize HBD as an alternative to mainstream social science.
HBD became a central theme in neoreactionary and alt-right circles, where it was used to argue against democracy, immigration, and racial equality policies.

WHY IS HBD CONTROVERSIAL?

Scientific Misrepresentation

While human populations have genetic differences due to historical migration and adaptation, the vast majority of genetic variation occurs *within* populations rather than *between* them.
Intelligence, behavior, and social outcomes are influenced by a complex mix of genetics and environment.
HBD proponents exaggerate the genetic component while downplaying the effects of history, culture, education, and economics.

Use in Political Ideologies

HBD is frequently used to **justify racial determinism - claims that certain groups are biologically destined to be more successful or more prone to crime**, which has been a common talking point in white nationalist and neoreactionary discourse.

These arguments often lead to **policy implications that mirror past eugenics movements,** including calls for racial segregation, immigration bans, or an end to civil rights protections.

Flawed Methodology

Studies cited by HBD advocates often rely on discredited sources, biased sampling, and outdated racial classifications.
Many mainstream geneticists reject HBD's conclusions because they misapply findings from population genetics to social issues in a way that does not meet scientific rigor.

HBD presents itself as a "scientific" explanation for racial and social disparities, but it is widely criticized for being a repackaging of racial determinism under a new name. While human genetic diversity is a legitimate field of study, the way HBD is deployed in reactionary circles distorts scientific research to support ideological conclusions about governance, social order, and race relations.

The Problem With Yarvin's Racial Arguments

Yarvin's claims about race and governance **rest on selective historical examples and flawed assumptions.** He argues that ethnic homogeneity leads to political stability, but history does not support this claim as strongly as he suggests.

Many homogeneous societies have **suffered from internal conflict, civil wars, and economic collapse.** Japan, one of the most ethnically homogeneous nations in the world, has faced economic stagnation and political gridlock for decades. Meanwhile, diverse states like the United States and Singapore have thrived despite their multicultural populations.

His argument also ignores **how political institutions, economic systems, and historical contingencies shape national stability.** He treats racial and cultural homogeneity as the determining factor, but successful governance has more to do with **laws, infrastructure, education, and economic policy** than with the ethnic makeup of a country.

Furthermore, his reliance on human biodiversity theories **fails to account for the impact of history and environment** on political and economic development. Colonialism, industrialization, resource distribution, and historical inequalities all play a far larger role in shaping societies than Yarvin acknowledges. His framework assumes that **if some groups underperform others politically or economically, the cause must be biological,** rather than the result of historical or material conditions.

Is Diversity Actually Destabilizing?

Yarvin presents diversity as an inherent weakness, but in reality, many of the world's most successful states have been multicultural. The United States has remained one of the most powerful nations in history whilst being one of the most diverse. Empires like Rome and the Ottoman Empire thrived for centuries whilst governing multiethnic populations. Singapore, a tiny city-state with multiple linguistic and ethnic groups, has one of the most stable governments and strongest economies in the world.

The assumption that diversity automatically creates social strife ignores how institutions, governance, and civic culture can foster unity. While diversity can create challenges, it does not inevitably lead to political collapse. It is how diversity is managed, not diversity itself, that determines stability.

Yarvin's argument also assumes that ethnic or cultural homogeneity guarantees social harmony, but history suggests otherwise. Nations with a single dominant ethnic group have still faced class conflict, regional tensions, and ideological divisions. Stability is not simply a question of race or culture but of governance, leadership, and economic opportunity.

Does Yarvin Provide a Solution?

While Yarvin critiques diversity, he does not offer a clear solution beyond implying that **Western nations should limit immigration and restore a strong, unified national identity.** However, this raises practical and ethical questions. If he believes multicultural societies are inherently unstable, does that mean diverse nations should break apart? Should governments enforce ethnic or cultural homogeneity? Should immigrants be forcibly repatriated? He does not answer these questions directly.

Instead, he frames his argument as a **warning** - a claim that Western countries are on a path to collapse because they have abandoned their historical identities. His solution is implied rather than stated: that governments should either **restrict diversity or allow a ruling elite to govern without concern for democratic representation.**

Key Takeaways

Yarvin argues that **diverse societies are inherently unstable** and that political systems function best when they govern a population with a shared racial or cultural background.

He engages with **human biodiversity theories,**

suggesting that biological differences between ethnic groups explain differences in political and economic success.

His argument assumes that **ethnic homogeneity guarantees social trust and stability,** but history provides many examples of homogeneous societies facing internal strife and collapse.

He ignores how **institutions, governance, and economic policies shape national stability,** reducing complex social dynamics to simplistic racial explanations.

His critique of multiculturalism **lacks a clear solution** beyond implying that states should limit immigration and strengthen national identity.

While Yarvin frames his views as an objective analysis of history and governance, his reliance on outdated racial theories and selective historical examples weakens his argument.

TESTING THE FRAMEWORK

Historical examples reveal fundamental problems with Yarvin's racial theories:

Modern Multicultural Success Stories

- Singapore transformed from a poor, riot-torn colony in 1965 into one of the world's most stable and prosperous nations while maintaining Chinese, Malay, and Indian populations. Its institutions actively manage diversity through housing policy, language rights, and representation requirements.
- Canada developed successful federal multiculturalism policies, officially recognizing both English and French languages while integrating waves of immigration. Its

constitutional framework and institutional design explicitly balance diversity with unity.

- Switzerland's canton system allows French, German, Italian, and Romansh regions significant autonomy while maintaining national cohesion through federal institutions and direct democracy.

Historical Empire Management

- The Roman Empire sustained power for centuries by extending citizenship rights to conquered peoples and allowing local autonomy in religion and customs, directly contradicting Yarvin's claim that diversity inevitably leads to collapse.
- The Ottoman Empire's millet system successfully managed diverse religious and ethnic groups for hundreds of years by granting them internal autonomy while maintaining central authority.
- The Habsburg Empire balanced multiple ethnic groups through sophisticated administrative systems and cultural autonomy, though it ultimately collapsed due to war and nationalism rather than diversity itself.

The Homogeneous State Myth

- Japan, despite near-perfect ethnic homogeneity, has faced decades of economic stagnation and political gridlock, showing that ethnic unity doesn't guarantee stability or success.
- North Korea represents perhaps the world's most ethnically homogeneous and culturally unified state, yet produces catastrophic governance outcomes.

- Northern European states often cited as examples of homogeneous success actually demonstrate the importance of institutions over ethnicity - their stability comes from strong social democracy rather than ethnic unity.

CONNECT THE DOTS

Consider these questions:

- How do successful multicultural states maintain stability?
- What role do institutions play versus demographic factors?
- How have historical empires managed diverse populations?
- Why do some homogeneous societies still face internal conflict?
- Does ethnic or cultural homogeneity actually lead to better governance, or does stability come from strong institutions and economic policies?
- If diversity is a weakness, why have some of the most successful states in history been multicultural?
- Is Yarvin's argument about race based on evidence, or is it an attempt to justify elite rule through biological determinism?

Examine three historical cases of diverse governance. For each, analyze:

1. How the state managed diversity
2. What institutions proved effective
3. Where conflicts emerged and why

4. How stability was maintained or lost

Some examples to consider:

- Singapore's multicultural policies
- Ottoman millet system
- Swiss canton model
- Roman citizenship approach
- Habsburg Empire
- Modern Canada

Looking Ahead

For the next chapter on Gender, Patriarchy, and the Role of Women, consider:

- How do Yarvin's views on racial hierarchy parallel his gender arguments?
- Does his "biological determinism" about race mirror his claims about gender?
- How does his ideal of homogeneous rule extend to gender roles?
- What role do women play in his vision of "natural" social hierarchies?
- How does his critique of diversity intersect with his views on feminism?
- Can his arguments about "social cohesion" be separated from traditional patriarchy?

Gender, Patriarchy, and the Role of Women

Yarvin argues that feminism has undermined political and social stability by eroding traditional gender roles. In his view, societies that emphasize gender equality prioritize sentimentality over competence, leading to weaker governance, economic inefficiency, and social fragmentation. Like his other arguments, he presents this critique not as a moral position but as a technical analysis of governance optimization.

Why Does Yarvin Oppose Gender Equality?

His critique of feminism rests on several key claims:

- Women's political participation shifts governance toward emotional rather than rational decision-making
- Traditional gender roles evolved to optimize society

- Women's entry into politics and workforce has weakened necessary hierarchies
- Gender equality undermines social stability and economic efficiency

Rather than making explicitly moral or religious arguments, Yarvin frames these as historical inevitabilities. He claims to be describing natural social patterns rather than prescribing ideological positions.

Gender, Patriarchy, and the Role of Women

Yarvin argues that feminism has undermined political and social stability by eroding traditional gender roles. In his view, societies that emphasize gender equality prioritize sentimentality over competence, leading to weaker governance, economic inefficiency, and social fragmentation. Like his other arguments, he presents this critique not as a moral position but as a technical analysis of social optimization.

What's Yarvin's View of Gender?

His critique of feminism rests on several key claims:

- Biological differences between men and women naturally produce different social roles
- Traditional gender arrangements evolved to optimize society's function
- Modern feminism disrupts natural hierarchies and creates instability
- Women's nature makes them better suited for domestic rather than public roles

- Female traits (empathy, care-focused thinking) become destructive when applied to governance

Rather than making explicitly moral or religious arguments, Yarvin frames these as historical inevitabilities. He claims to be describing natural patterns rather than prescribing ideological positions.

The Domestic Sphere

Yarvin believes women's traditional role - managing households, supporting husbands, and raising children - created stable social foundations. He argues that feminism's push for workplace equality has undermined this essential social function. In his view:

- Female workforce participation weakens family structures
- Children suffer from lack of maternal care
- Domestic expertise is devalued by feminist ideology
- Society loses stability when women abandon traditional roles

He presents this domestic focus not as oppression but as an optimal division of labor that evolved naturally over time.

Women in the Workforce

According to Yarvin, mass entry of women into the workforce has:

- Reduced wages by doubling the labor supply
- Created inefficient workplace accommodations

- Prioritized equality over merit in hiring
- Shifted organizational culture toward "feminine" values
- Undermined male authority in professional settings

Education and Achievement

Yarvin argues that pushing women toward higher education and professional achievement:

- Delays or prevents family formation
- Creates unrealistic expectations
- Wastes resources on career paths women will abandon for motherhood
- Undermines natural gender dynamics in mate selection
- Produces unhappiness by fighting biological imperatives

The Biological Argument

Like his racial theories, Yarvin's gender views rely heavily on biological determinism:

- Claims women are naturally more emotional and less rational
- Argues female brains are optimized for different tasks than male brains
- Suggests physical differences justify social hierarchies
- Uses evolutionary psychology to justify traditional roles

- Treats gender differences as immutable rather than cultural

Testing These Claims

Historical and contemporary evidence contradicts Yarvin's gender theories:

Modern Economies: The most successful economies have high female workforce participation. Nations with greater gender equality consistently show better economic performance and stability.

Leadership Examples: Leaders like Merkel, Thatcher, and Meir demonstrated that women can govern with strategic rationality. Their success contradicts claims about feminine emotionality undermining governance.

Family Structures: Societies with greater gender equality often have more stable family structures, not less. Nordic countries combine high female workforce participation with high birth rates and family stability.

Educational Impact: Female education correlates strongly with societal health metrics, including child welfare, economic growth, and political stability.

Core Contradictions

Yarvin's gender framework contains several fundamental flaws:

- He treats current gender roles as natural while ignoring their historical development. Women's domestic focus is relatively recent - historically, women performed significant economic labor alongside domestic duties.
- His biological determinism ignores vast evidence of cultural influence on gender expression.

Societies throughout history have defined gender roles differently.

- His argument that women naturally prefer domestic roles conflicts with demonstrated female achievement when barriers are removed.

Connect the Dots

Consider these questions:

- How do successful societies integrate women into public life?
- What evidence supports or refutes biological determinism?
- How have gender roles actually evolved historically?
- Why do more gender-equal societies often show better outcomes?

Examine three cases of changing gender roles. For each, analyze:

- What drove the changes
- How society adapted
- What outcomes resulted
- What resistance emerged

Some examples to consider:

- Post-WWII workforce changes
- Nordic gender equality policies
- Japanese workforce modernization
- Soviet women in industry
- Modern professional sectors

- Traditional agricultural societies

Looking Ahead

- For the next chapter on Exit vs. Voice, consider:
- How do gender dynamics affect political participation?
- What role do women play in societal change?
- How does gender intersect with other forms of hierarchy?
- Can Yarvin's ideal system accommodate modern gender realities?
- How do power structures maintain or challenge gender roles?

Exit vs. Voice - Reform is Impossible

Yarvin argues that trying to reform democracy from within is futile. The system, he claims, is designed to protect itself from meaningful change, no matter who is elected or what policies they attempt to enact. Instead of political activism, he advocates for "exit" rather than "voice" - withdrawing from the system entirely to build alternative structures rather than trying to fix democracy through conventional means.

What Does Yarvin Mean by Exit?

Borrowing from political scientist Albert O. Hirschman, Yarvin presents two options for dealing with failed systems:

Voice: Attempting change from within through voting, protest, or reform

Exit: Abandoning broken institutions to create alternatives

He argues that voice is useless because:

- Democratic institutions are self-reinforcing and resist real change
- Elections don't matter since power lies with unelected bureaucracies
- The system absorbs and neutralizes dissent
- Reform efforts only strengthen existing power structures

Instead, Yarvin advocates complete exit through:

- Seasteading (floating city-states in international waters)
- Private cities and special economic zones
- Cryptocurrency and digital sovereignty
- Parallel institutions outside state control

WHY DOES YARVIN THINK REFORM IS IMPOSSIBLE?

Even when outsiders win elections, Yarvin argues they're constrained by:

- Permanent bureaucracy that shapes policy regardless of elected leadership
- Legal system that blocks changes threatening institutional power
- Media and academia that enforce ideological boundaries
- Financial systems that limit radical economic changes
- International institutions that punish non-compliance

He points to examples of populist leaders who

campaigned against the system but were effectively neutralized once in office, either through institutional resistance or by being co-opted into existing power structures.

The Mechanics of Exit

Yarvin proposes several concrete exit strategies:

Seasteading: Building sovereign floating cities in international waters. This would theoretically allow for:

- Complete legal autonomy
- New governance experiments
- Tax and regulatory independence
- Protection from existing state power

Charter Cities: Creating new jurisdictions with separate legal systems, like:

- Special economic zones with different rules
- Private cities with corporate governance
- Autonomous regions with independent policies
- Startup societies testing new social models

Digital Exit: Using technology to bypass state control through:

- Cryptocurrency to escape financial systems
- Encrypted communications networks
- Decentralized organizations
- Alternative economic structures

Why Exit Fails

Historical examples reveal consistent patterns of failure:

Resource Problems:

- Seasteading requires massive capital investment
- New cities need existing infrastructure
- Alternative systems depend on global trade
- Technology still relies on physical infrastructure

State Resistance:

- Micronations are never recognized
- Separatist movements face military action
- Financial systems are heavily regulated
- States control physical infrastructure

Practical Limitations:

- Most people can't abandon their lives
- New systems face same human problems
- External pressures don't disappear
- Power structures reproduce themselves

The Reality Check

Yarvin's exit strategy faces several insurmountable problems:

Scale: Only a tiny elite could potentially exit. The vast majority of people remain trapped in existing systems, making exit a solution only for the privileged few.

Infrastructure: New societies require massive physical infrastructure - ports, power, internet, defense - all controlled by existing states.

Recognition: International systems of trade, travel, and diplomacy require state recognition. No exit project has overcome this barrier.

Resources: Building parallel institutions requires enormous resources, which paradoxically must be accumulated within the very system being rejected.

Testing the Framework

Several problems emerge with Yarvin's exit theory:

The Physical Exit Problem

Most people cannot simply abandon their country or political system. Creating new societies requires enormous resources. Even successful examples like Hong Kong, Dubai, or Singapore relied heavily on existing state structures and global trade networks.

The State Resistance Problem

Governments actively prevent exit. They don't allow their tax base or labor force to simply walk away. History shows breakaway states and self-governing communities face sanctions, political pressure, or military intervention.

The Governance Problem

Exit doesn't solve fundamental challenges of leadership, stability, and corruption. Yarvin assumes alternative systems will function better but doesn't explain how they'll handle dissent, succession, or long-term stability.

Core Contradictions

Yarvin's exit framework contains several fatal flaws:

- He treats democracy as uniquely resistant to change while ignoring historical evidence of major political transformations achieved through "voice."

- His vision of exit assumes new political entities can operate free from existing power structures, ignoring economic pressures and geopolitical realities.
- His dismissal of reform contradicts historical examples where internal pressure produced significant change.
- Exit requires cooperation from existing power structures - the very ones Yarvin claims make reform impossible.
- His focus on elite exit ignores the fate of the majority who cannot exit, undermining his critique of democratic legitimacy.

CONNECT THE DOTS

Consider these questions:

- How have societies actually achieved major political change?
- What determines whether voice or exit strategies succeed?
- Can parallel institutions truly operate outside state control?
- What happens when states actively resist exit attempts?

Examine three historical cases of attempted exit. For each, analyze:

- What conditions led to the attempt
- How existing powers responded
- Whether it succeeded or failed
- What factors determined the outcome

Some examples to consider:

- American Revolution
- Confederate secession
- Singapore's separation from Malaysia
- Rhodesia's UDI
- Modern seasteading attempts
- Free city movements

Looking Ahead

For the next chapter on Yarvin's influence, consider:

- How do tech elites interpret his exit framework?
- Why does Silicon Valley find exit attractive?
- What role does technology play in enabling exit?
- How do different groups adapt his ideas?
- What makes exit appealing to those with power?

The Silicon Valley Connection

Yarvin's most direct influence is in Silicon Valley, particularly through Peter Thiel, though many of their shared ideas have deeper libertarian roots:

Many concepts attributed to Yarvin originated in James Dale Davidson and Lord William Rees-Mogg's *The Sovereign Individual* (1997). Thiel and Yarvin both draw heavily from this work, particularly:

- The concept of "sovereign individuals" escaping state control
- The prediction that technology would enable exit from traditional governance
- The vision of charter cities and independent zones
- The idea that democracy is incompatible with technological progress

Thiel's actions reflect these shared influences:

- His Founders Fund seeks to enable "sovereign individuals"

- He invests in seasteading and charter cities
- His essay "The Education of a Libertarian" combines Yarvin's critique of democracy with Sovereign Individual concepts
- His companies (Palantir, PayPal) implement the corporate-governance model both writers advocate

Yarvin's ideas often reframe and build upon existing libertarian and anti-democratic thought rather than originating entirely new concepts.

Beyond Thiel, Yarvin's ideas manifest in Silicon Valley through:

- Startup founders adopting "CEO as sovereign" models
- VC rhetoric about "breaking away from legacy systems"
- Tech leaders' emphasis on parallel institutions
- The industry's broader rejection of democratic decision-making

Recent Tech Industry Impact

Yarvin's ideas increasingly shape Silicon Valley's anti-democratic turn:

Marc Andreessen's "Techno-Optimist Manifesto" echoes Yarvin's critique of state control over innovation and his belief that tech elites should have more power. a16z's broader stance against regulation and democratic oversight closely aligns with Yarvin's views about elite competence versus democratic interference.

Elon Musk's statements about "unelected bureaucrats" and his criticism of regulatory agencies mirror Yarvin's "Cathedral" concept, though Musk likely draws these ideas indirectly through tech culture rather than from Yarvin directly.

Political Sphere

Yarvin's influence extends into mainstream politics through:

- JD Vance, who received significant backing from Thiel and has met with Yarvin
- Blake Masters' campaign, which explicitly used Yarvin-influenced messaging about institutional control
- Trump's attacks on the "deep state," which parallel Yarvin's Cathedral concept though through different language
- The broader "New Right" movement incorporating his critique of democratic institutions

HOW IDEAS TRANSLATE

Each sphere adapts Yarvin's ideas differently:

Tech Elites transform Yarvin's monarchy into corporate governance theory. They reframe his call for absolute rule into familiar startup concepts: the visionary founder-CEO, the lean organization, the disruptive innovation. When Yarvin talks about a sovereign ruler, they hear Mark Zuckerberg's total control of Facebook. His critique of democracy becomes their frustration with regulation and "red tape." They embrace his exit strategy through projects like seasteading and charter cities, seeing them as startup opportunities to "disrupt" governance.

Political Figures transform Yarvin's ideas into populist critiques of institutional power. When Yarvin talks about the Cathedral controlling society regardless of elections, they hear the "deep state" undermining elected officials. His call for elite rule gets repackaged as attacks on "unelected bureaucrats" and "expert" overreach. JD Vance and Blake Masters, backed by Thiel, translate Yarvin's technical critique of democratic institutions into voter-friendly language about "taking back control" from federal agencies. Trump's attacks on the FBI, intelligence agencies, and career civil servants echo Yarvin's framework without his theoretical underpinning. Even politicians who've never read Yarvin end up channeling his ideas through the broader "New Right" movement's adoption of his institutional analysis.

The Intellectual Right takes Yarvin's framework and wraps it in academic language and traditional conservative thought. His critique of the "Cathedral" becomes their analysis of institutional capture. His call for monarchy gets repackaged as "post-liberal" governance or "common good constitutionalism." They're less interested in his technical solutions and more focused on his dismantling of democratic legitimacy. Writers like Patrick Deneen and Adrian Vermeule may not cite Yarvin directly, but their critiques of liberalism mirror his core arguments.

Online Movements strip Yarvin's complex theories down to easily shared concepts. His careful critique of democratic systems becomes simplified anti-democracy memes. His analysis of power structures gets reduced to conspiracy theories about elite control. While these groups often miss his nuance, they spread his core ideas widely. They transform his academic writing into provocative slogans and engaging content, though often at the cost of his original meaning.

From Theory to Practice

While Yarvin's direct influence remains limited, his ideas shape discourse:

Tech Implementation:

- "Sovereign individual" cryptocurrency projects
- Private city initiatives like Prospera in Honduras
- "Democracy-free" corporate structures
- Digital exit through Web3 and blockchain

Political, Religious & Intellectual Applications:

- Patrick Deneen's "Why Liberalism Failed"
- Vermeule's "common good constitutionalism"
- National Conservative movement's anti-liberal turn
- New Right critiques of democratic institutions and democracy
- Post-liberal Catholic movement
- New Right media

Online Manifestations:

- "Dark Enlightenment" communities
- Accelerationist tech discourse
- Anti-democracy meme culture
- "Based" governance discussions

POST-LIBERAL CATHOLIC MOVEMENT

Post-liberal Catholic thinkers like Adrian Vermeule, Patrick Deneen, and Sohrab Ahmari reject both liberal democracy and modern Catholic accommodation with it. While mainstream American Catholics typically accept religious pluralism and separation of church and state, post-liberal Catholics advocate using state power to promote Catholic social teaching and moral order.

This movement is often critical of Pope Francis, viewing his emphasis on mercy, inclusion, and dialogue with modernity as compromising Catholic tradition. They tend to align with traditionalist Catholic groups and often prefer the Latin Mass, though they're not necessarily connected to specific organizations like Opus Dei. Their key departure from mainstream Catholic teaching isn't about doctrine per se, but about how Catholicism should interact with modern society: where Vatican II and subsequent Catholic teaching has sought dialogue with modern democracy and pluralism, post-liberals argue for a more confrontational approach.

Rhetorical Evolution

Yarvin has strategically rebranded his message over time:

Early Period (2007-2014):

- Openly monarchist
- Explicitly anti-democratic
- Heavy focus on race and IQ
- Dense, academic style

Middle Period (2014-2019):

- Shift to "corporate governance"
- More coded language
- Focus on institutional critique
- Tech-friendly framing

Recent Period (2019-present):

- "Governance engineering"
- Mainstream conservative outreach
- Silicon Valley vocabulary

- "Post-political" positioning

Measuring Influence

Despite growing reach, Yarvin's actual impact faces clear limits:

Practical Barriers:

- No government has adopted neocameralist models
- Exit projects remain mostly theoretical
- Tech elites continue working within system
- Parallel institutions still depend on state power

Ideological Dilution:

- Complex theories become simplified slogans
- Different groups cherry-pick elements
- Original framework gets distorted
- Strategic rebranding weakens core ideas

Connect the Dots

Consider these questions:

- How do ideas transform as they spread?
- Why do different groups interpret Yarvin differently?
- What makes his ideas appealing to elites?
- How does influence translate to action?

Examine three cases of Yarvin's influence. For each, analyze:

- How ideas were adopted

- What elements were emphasized
- What got lost in translation
- What practical effects emerged

Some examples to consider:

- Thiel's political projects
- Charter city movements
- Cryptocurrency communities
- New Right media outlets
- Post-liberal intellectuals
- Tech startup culture

Looking Ahead

For the final chapter on Yarvin's future influence, consider:

- Will his ideas move beyond theory?
- How might different spheres develop his thought?
- What happens as his influence grows?
- Can his framework survive mainstreaming?
- How do his ideas shape future movements?

Yarvin: What Now?

For Yarvin's vision to materialize, it would require **the dismantling of democratic governance in favor of a corporate-state model.**

From Theory to Practice

What would actual implementation of Yarvin's ideas look like? Consider a scenario where a tech billionaire is given unilateral control over federal systems:

- Access to all government data and systems
- Authority to shut down agencies at will
- Power to purge the federal workforce
- Control over treasury and payment systems

This mirrors Yarvin's vision of governance as corporate takeover:

- A sovereign executive with total control
- Dismantling of bureaucratic structures

- Replacement of career civil servants with loyal operators
- Direct control of state financial mechanisms

The scenario illustrates how Yarvin's seemingly abstract ideas about "corporate governance" could materialize through existing power structures. Rather than building parallel institutions, a sovereign executive could simply absorb and restructure current ones - exactly as a CEO might restructure an acquired company.

This also demonstrates why tech elites find Yarvin appealing: they already run their companies this way and see no reason why governance should be different. The idea of someone "fixing government like he fixed XYZ Company" represents exactly the kind of corporate-state merger Yarvin advocates.

Paths to Implementation

Tech Enclaves:

- Charter cities and special economic zones
- Corporate governance experiments
- Private city projects
- Digital sovereignty zones

Political Crisis:

- Economic collapse creating demand for alternatives
- Democratic dysfunction leading to elite consolidation
- Technological disruption enabling new governance models

- Social instability driving authoritarian solutions

Gradual Infiltration:

- Tech companies expanding governance roles
- Private institutions replacing state functions
- Corporate structures absorbing political power
- Elite networks adopting neocameralist principles

The rise of techno-authoritarian enclaves.

Cities like Dubai, Singapore, and even Silicon Valley-adjacent projects (such as charter cities and seasteading experiments) function with highly centralized authority and limited democratic participation. While they are not fully neocameralist, they operate under the logic that governance should prioritize efficiency and elite decision-making.

Special economic zones as experimental governance models.

Certain nations are increasingly embracing privatized governance structures in the form of SEZs (Special Economic Zones), where governments grant vast autonomy to corporations. Yarvin's framework could theoretically evolve through these types of experiments.

Big Tech exerting greater control over political and social life.

Companies like Amazon, Google, and Meta already govern massive digital spaces and wield regulatory-like power over speech, commerce, and online behavior. Some aspects of neocameralism - particularly centralized corporate governance - are already functioning in digital spaces, suggesting a slow drift toward Yarvin's ideas in practice.

What is Holding Back Yarvin's Vision?

Despite his growing influence, there are still obstacles preventing Yarvin's ideas from becoming reality.

Democratic institutions still hold legitimacy. As of February 2025, it is unclear whether that is still the case. While Yarvin argues that democracy is an illusion, it remains a deeply ingrained system of governance. Even where dissatisfaction with democracy is high, few are calling for **its outright replacement with a sovereign CEO.** This shift may be underway in the United States.

Second, **his model of government lacks a clear transition path.** While Yarvin critiques democracy effectively, he does not provide a clear roadmap for how societies should shift from democratic rule to corporate governance. This makes his ideas intellectually provocative but practically difficult to implement.

BUT, **elite support for Yarvin's vision is no longer mostly theoretical.** Certain tech billionaires are sympathetic to his critiques of democracy and have **made serious efforts to dismantle the existing system.** They no longer appear interested in working within existing political structures, instead, they appear to be attempting to create an entirely new system.

Yarvin's Recent Evolution - Is He Softening or Strategizing?

As Yarvin's audience has grown, **his rhetoric has changed.** In his early years, writing as Mencius Moldbug, he was explicit about monarchy as a superior system of government. Now, he presents himself less as a revolutionary and more as a detached observer of political decline.

His shift in tone raises the question: Is he softening his stance, or simply refining his strategy?

Yarvin's recent public appearances suggest **he is strategically adjusting his messaging to appeal to a wider audience.** Instead of directly advocating for the abolition of democracy, **he now frames his ideas in terms of pragmatism and efficiency.** By using **corporate governance metaphors instead of outright monarchist language,** he makes his ideas more palatable to those who might resist authoritarianism but still distrust democratic dysfunction.

This rhetorical evolution mirrors how Yarvin has distanced himself from the more extreme reactionary movements that have co-opted his ideas. While his influence is undeniable, he is careful to avoid direct association with groups that promote racial nationalism or overt authoritarianism.

The Possibility of a Crisis-Driven Adoption of Yarvin's Ideas

While Yarvin's vision has not yet been implemented, **major political or economic crises could create conditions where his ideas gain traction.** If Western democracies continue to struggle with instability, gridlock, and perceived inefficiency, **elite calls for a more centralized, competent ruling structure may become more appealing.**

Several historical precedents show how political systems can shift dramatically in times of crisis:

- The fall of the Roman Republic led to the rise of the Roman Empire, as elites lost faith in the

democratic process and consolidated power under a single ruler.
- WWI and The Great Depression weakened faith in liberal democracy, leading to the rise of authoritarian leaders across Europe.
- China's transition from Maoist communism to state-controlled capitalism created a hybrid model of centralized executive authority with corporate efficiency, echoing some elements of Yarvin's neocameralist vision.

If a major economic collapse, technological upheaval, or widespread political dysfunction occurs in the West, the demand for alternative governance models could grow. In such a scenario, Yarvin's ideas might move from the realm of theoretical discussion to actual implementation.

Will Yarvin's Ideas Continue to Spread?

Even if neocameralism is never fully realized, Yarvin's influence is likely to persist in more subtle ways. His framing of democracy as an inefficient and self-reinforcing system has already shaped political discourse among tech elites, reactionary intellectuals, and sections of the populist right.

We can expect to see continued experiments in private governance, corporate cities, and decentralized digital economies that align with elements of Yarvin's vision. Even if his ideas never become the dominant political framework, they will continue to shape discussions about the future of governance.

Connect the Dots

- Could Yarvin's vision gain more traction if Western democracies experience severe crises?
- Is his shift in rhetoric a sign that he is moderating, or is he simply rebranding his ideas to reach a broader audience?
- Are aspects of neocameralism already emerging in special economic zones, big tech governance, or corporate influence over policy?

"An Open Letter to Open-Minded Progressives"

"An *Open Letter...*" was written by Yarvin under the pseudonym Moldbug.

Part 1: Progressivism as a Belief System

Moldbug opens by comparing progressivism to Catholicism, arguing that both are systems of *belief* rather than *rational* perspectives.

He asserts that progressives trust that their worldview accurately reflects reality, but most have only secondhand knowledge of history, government, and economics, relying on trusted institutions rather than direct experience.

Progressivism functions like a religion, requiring trust in authoritative institutions the way Catholicism requires faith in spiritual authority.

Moldbug argues that he lost his trust in progressive institutions, similar to how David Mamet renounced his "brain-dead liberal" beliefs, though Mamet made the mistake of embracing mainstream conservatism instead.

Rejecting progressivism does not require embracing

conservatism. Instead of two competing worldviews - one rational, one delusional - Moldbug suggests a third possibility: both are mass delusions.

Rather than a battle between truth and ignorance, American democracy may be a **contest between two political machines**, each feeding its followers narratives that reinforce its own power rather than reflecting reality.

Progressivism, like conservatism, is shaped by institutional incentives rather than an objective pursuit of truth. If falsehoods replicate more effectively than truths within progressive institutions, progressives will believe them just as conservatives believe Fox News misinformation.

To truly question progressivism, one must challenge its foundational institutions, not just identify minor factual errors.

Progressivism is not just a political ideology but **America's dominant intellectual tradition**, evolving continuously from early New England Puritanism to modern liberalism. **To doubt progressivism is to challenge the entire trajectory of American history.**

Part 2: Historical Anomalies That Challenge Progressivism

Moldbug introduces three **historical contradictions** that progressivism struggles to explain:

The Third World Paradox

> Postcolonial independence movements are celebrated as victories for freedom, yet they often resulted in **civil war, poverty, corruption, and institutional collapse.** Why is this still considered progress?

Despite these outcomes, it remains politically unacceptable to suggest that colonial governments may have been **more competent and effective** than the postcolonial regimes that replaced them.

The Asymmetry of Nationalism

Some nationalist movements (Vietnamese, Algerian, African liberation movements) are **praised**, while others (Southern nationalism, German nationalism) are **demonized.**
Why is nationalism acceptable when it aligns with progressive institutions but condemned when it resists them?
Even within the U.S., **black nationalism is encouraged**, while white or Southern nationalism is treated as inherently dangerous.

The Moral Hierarchy of Totalitarianism

Nazi crimes are considered uniquely evil, yet communist regimes - responsible for even greater mass murder - are excused or ignored.
Fascism is seen as the ultimate evil because it was the **enemy of progressive institutions**, whereas communism, despite its atrocities, is treated as a **misguided ally** rather than an existential threat.
Moldbug argues that these contradictions make sense **if progressivism is not about truth but about maintaining institutional dominance.**

PART 3: THE ROLE OF THE "INTERNATIONAL COMMUNITY" AS A PREDATORY FORCE

Moldbug challenges the idea that the **"international community"** is a benevolent force. Instead, he argues that it functions as a **global power structure**, using moral rhetoric to justify its own expansion and control.

The Cold War powers - particularly the U.S. and its allies - did not "liberate" the Third World but conquered it under the pretext of decolonization, installing governments that were politically dependent on Western institutions.

Postcolonial regimes often **did not govern independently** but remained **financially and politically reliant on Western aid and approval.**

Moldbug introduces the idea of "**muppet states**" - regimes that appear independent but are effectively controlled by outside forces, much like the Warsaw Pact countries were Soviet satellites.

Many nationalist movements were not truly organic revolutions but were backed by Western elites who saw them as useful in dismantling old power structures that resisted progressivism.

Moldbug likens this process to the liberal revolutions of the 19th century, where reactionary governments were toppled under the banner of liberty, only to be replaced by regimes more aligned with international power networks.

Thus, the so-called **"independence" movements** of the 20th century were often just a **continuation of empire under a new name** - one where control was exerted through institutions, funding, and ideology rather than direct colonial rule.

Moldbug closes this section by noting that **fascism was the only reactionary movement that fought back** against the progressive world order. Unlike traditional monarchies or conservative regimes, which were gradually dismantled, fascist states actively resisted.

For this reason, progressivism treats fascism as uniquely evil, while communist regimes - despite their similar totalitarianism - are excused or even romanticized.

By connecting these historical patterns, Moldbug presents an alternative history of the 20th century, one where progressivism is not a force for truth and justice but a hegemonic power structure that eliminates rivals, absorbs useful movements, and sustains itself through selective moral outrage.

The Jacobite History of the World

The Seed of Doubt

Moldbug acknowledges that his argument has not yet converted the reader from progressivism to reactionary thought. Instead, he sees his task as planting small seeds of doubt, gently watering them to encourage a slow realization rather than an immediate transformation.

The **progressive worldview**, shared by both conservatives and leftists in modern America, is filled with **paradoxes and contradictions** that require explanation.

One such contradiction is the **end of colonialism**, which is celebrated as a victory for humanity, yet in many cases resulted in **economic decline, civil war, and authoritarian rule**. The progressive mind must reconcile these two opposing realities, often concluding that the transition was a **tragic victory** rather than outright failure.

Moldbug argues that history is often shrouded in mysticism, much like religious doctrine. While progressives see their worldview as rational and objective, many of their core beliefs function more like dogma than reasoned conclusions.

The Role of the Cathedral and the Manufacturing of "Responsible" Opinion

Moldbug examines the **progressive role in shaping public discourse**, using the media's coverage of figures like Robert Mugabe as an example.

Journalists and intellectuals **never take responsibility for their role in shaping political realities**, despite the fact that they influence the beliefs and actions of the public. They frame their role as passive observers, yet their narratives shape history just as much as politicians do.

Progressives believe in "responsible journalism," but Moldbug argues that this is simply another way of saying that **journalism exists to promote progressive values**, rather than to seek truth in an objective way.

Similarly, progressive moral contradictions - such as how a long-time member of a racially radical church could become the symbol of racial unity - are not treated as genuine mysteries that require resolution. Instead, these contradictions are smoothed over by the intellectual class, because **progressivism is not about coherence, but power and narrative control.**

The Reactionary Worldview

Defining the Political Spectrum

Moldbug offers a historical framework for understanding the political left and right, arguing that these categories predate the French Revolution and remain consistent across history.

- **Left-wing movements** - whether the Protestant Reformation, the French Revolution, or 20th-century progressivism - **are always about**

disrupting existing power structures and redistributing authority.

- **Right-wing movements** - whether monarchism, Catholicism, or modern reactionaries - **believe in stability, order, and hierarchy** as fundamental principles of governance.

This linear spectrum of left and right is a rare phenomenon in history. Unlike other domains of thought (such as music or literature), political philosophy consistently arranges itself along this single axis, which suggests that politics follows a deeper, structural logic rather than merely reflecting the whims of history.

The Reactionary Definition of Government

Moldbug defines **reactionary thought** as the belief in **order, stability, and security** - all of which he treats as synonyms.

The **purpose of government is to impose order** and maintain security. Reactionaries believe that sovereignty is a question of who actually holds power, not who should hold power in some moral or philosophical sense.

Legitimacy, in the reactionary view, is **not about fairness or justice** but about **who actually rules effectively**. This is why reactionaries do not believe in popular sovereignty, since public opinion can be easily manipulated and does not guarantee competent governance.

Moldbug argues that many right-wing movements fail because they embrace weak, half-measures rather than full reactionary principles.

A **true reactionary government does not believe in democracy or universal suffrage,** but instead believes in

clear, unambiguous rule - whether by monarchy, corporate governance, or some other structured, hierarchical system.

WHY PROGRESSIVISM WINS

The W-Force: Why the Left Always Wins

Moldbug introduces the **W-Force**, a mysterious historical tendency for **leftist movements to gain power over time**, while right-wing movements gradually retreat or disappear.

This is evident in how:

- Monarchies gave way to constitutional monarchies
- Constitutional monarchies gave way to parliamentary democracy
- Parliamentary democracy shifted from aristocratic control to mass democracy
- Mass democracy then embraced socialism and central planning

Even when the right temporarily wins, as in the case of conservatism, it merely preserves the previous leftist victory rather than rolling it back.

Moldbug describes **modern conservatism as a failed movement**, because it does not resist progressivism, but merely slows it down. It only opposes the next leftward move, never undoing the last one.

This is why **reactionaries must reject conservatism** - it is not a genuine counterforce to progressivism, but merely a delayed version of the same process.

The Myth of Progress

Progressives believe in Whig history - the idea that **history is a continuous march toward progress, enlightenment, and justice.**

This belief assumes that all past reactionary resistance was futile and wrong, while all progressive victories were inevitable and good.

Moldbug argues that this is circular reasoning - progress is good because it happens, and it happens because it is good.

This leads to the mystification of history, where modern people assume that their moral standards are superior to those of the past, simply because they are newer.

Moldbug challenges the idea that progress is inevitable, suggesting instead that it is a process of accumulating power under new ideological justifications, rather than a movement toward truth.

The Cathedral: Spontaneous Ideological Coordination

How the Progressive Elite Rules Without Conspiracy

Moldbug introduces the concept of **the Cathedral**, which refers to the self-organizing system of universities, media, and intellectuals that define progressive thought.

Unlike a totalitarian regime, where the state explicitly dictates what can be said, the **Cathedral operates through spontaneous consensus** - universities and journalists are not centrally controlled, yet they all seem to believe the same things.

According to Moldbug, Harvard and Yale are not explicitly coordinated, but their output is ideologically indistinguishable.

The New York Times and The Washington Post may compete for readership, but they do not disagree on fundamental ideological questions.

Political scientists and historians at different institutions may have different specializations, but their conclusions align with the same progressive framework.

This spontaneous uniformity is what makes the Cathedral so powerful - it does not need coercion, because those who dissent are naturally excluded from positions of influence.

Why the Cathedral Always Moves Left

The Cathedral is **not neutral** - it is always shifting the Overton Window leftward.

This is because **progressive ideas create more power for the institutions that spread them**. If universities and journalists promoted reactionary thought, they would be advocating **for their own dissolution**.

Instead, progressivism advances ideas that **expand the role of academia and media** in governance, solidifying their position at the top of the intellectual hierarchy.

This is why the Cathedral:

- Advocates for bigger government, because intellectuals are the ones who guide policy.
- Supports identity politics and cultural progressivism, because these create endless new social issues for experts to analyze and regulate.
- Opposes reactionary thought, because reactionaries believe in order over intellectual control and reject the need for an elite class of progressive technocrats.

Conclusion: The Reactionary Answer to the W-Force

Moldbug argues that the only way to oppose the W-Force is to reject all progressive premises entirely.

Conservatives fail because they accept the legitimacy of progressive victories, only resisting further movement.

A **true reactionary movement** must:

- **Reject democracy as a stable form of government**
- **Reject universal suffrage as a sustainable model for decision-making**
- **Accept that order, rather than equality, is the highest political good**

The key lesson of history, according to Moldbug, is that half-measures do not stop the W-Force. Monarchies that tried to compromise with democracy eventually lost. Governments that conceded ground to socialism were eventually absorbed by it.

If reactionary thought is to survive, it must be unyielding - rejecting not just modern progressivism, but the entire lineage of leftist ideology that began with the Enlightenment.

Moldbug leaves the reader with a final question: Is progress really inevitable, or is it merely the result of power shifting hands under a new name?

PART 5: THE SHORTEST WAY TO WORLD PEACE

MOLDBUG'S REACTIONARY PLAN FOR WORLD PEACE

Moldbug begins by addressing **Charles Stross**, a science-fiction writer, using his open letter as a way to engage progressives in a radical alternative vision of global stability. He proposes a simple yet controversial plan:

The United States should recognize the sovereignty of every government on Earth and respect it according to the principles of classical international law.

On the surface, this may seem like a progressive position - non-intervention, self-determination, and respect for international law. However, Moldbug argues that it is actually the opposite: a **reactionary return to an older, more hierarchical system of global order.**

THE PROGRESSIVE MISUNDERSTANDING OF GOVERNMENT

Moldbug asserts that progressives misunderstand history and government much in the "same way" that Nazis "misunderstood"* Jews. Just as Nazi ideology distorted reality with paranoid, selective readings of history, **progressive ideology misinterprets power, sovereignty, and international relations.**

He challenges the **Whig theory of history**, which assumes that human civilization is on a constant march toward greater democracy and human rights. Instead, he suggests that **power moves in cycles**, and the current dominance of progressive values is not because they are inherently superior, but because they have been politically and institutionally successful.

Moldbug introduces a thought experiment:

If the Nazis had won World War II, they would have written a version of history that rationalized their victory and moral superiority.

---

* It should go without saying that these are not the views of the author of this guide and that the notion of miscomprehension is inadequate.

The same applies to the progressive world order, which dominates today. The way history is taught - where monarchy, hierarchy, and reactionary values are dismissed as inherently evil - is simply a function of who won the ideological war rather than an objective truth.

THE PROBLEM WITH MODERN INTERNATIONAL LAW

Moldbug contrasts classical international law with its modern progressive version.

- **Classical international law** (pre-World War I) was **practical, realist, and designed to maintain order** among sovereign states.
- **Modern international law** (post-World War II) is **moralistic, interventionist, and seeks to engineer global democracy**, often leading to endless conflict.

In classical international law, the **primary principle** was *uti possidetis* - the idea that **all governments that control territory are legitimate, regardless of ideology.**
This means:

- **No humanitarian interventions.**
- **No democracy-promotion.**
- **No meddling in other nations' internal affairs.**

Moldbug argues that World War I was the turning point, where the United States, influenced by progressive ideology, rejected classical international law in favor of moralistic interventionism. Woodrow Wilson's ideas of "making the world safe for democracy" transformed war from being about state interests to being about moral crusades - a shift that has led to a century of instability and interventionist wars.

How Insurgencies Work and Why They Exist

Moldbug explains that **insurgencies do not happen because of oppression or injustice**. Rather, they exist because **weak governments allow them to exist.**

- **No successful right-wing insurgencies exist.**
- **All insurgencies are left-wing or progressivist in nature, because they rely on antimilitarism to succeed.**

He argues that **warfare today is asymmetric**, not in the sense that one side is weaker, but in the sense that the insurgents use political means (propaganda, foreign sympathy) while the state is constrained by progressive norms.

Antimilitarism, a product of progressive thought, **prevents strong governments from crushing insurgencies quickly**. Instead, modern war is fought under legal constraints that favor guerrilla forces.

Moldbug gives a **hypothetical example**:

If Britain were invaded by Bolivia, but the British military was forced to treat Bolivian soldiers as criminals rather than enemy combatants, the Bolivians could easily win - not because they are stronger, but because the rules of engagement prevent Britain from fighting back effectively.

This, he argues, is exactly what happens in insurgencies today. The political wing of the insurgency (sympathetic intellectuals, media, progressive governments) protects the military wing from being wiped out.

The Reactionary Solution: A Return to Classical International Law

Moldbug's solution is to **end moralistic interventionism and restore classical international law**, which respects **de facto sovereignty** and allows states to govern as they see fit.

This would mean:

- No US military interventions (Iraq, Afghanistan, Libya, Ukraine, etc.).
- No global human rights enforcement.
- No democracy promotion.

Under this system:

- If a government is strong enough to hold power, it is legitimate.
- If a government is weak and loses power, it is not legitimate.
- Wars end when one side decisively wins, rather than being prolonged by foreign interference.

For example:

Israel and Palestine: Israel should be allowed to govern its land without interference, and Gaza should be treated as a sovereign state responsible for its own actions. If it attacks Israel, Israel has the right to respond with whatever force is necessary to stop the attacks.

Iraq & Afghanistan: The US should never have attempted "nation-building" and instead either ruled Iraq as a colony or left it alone entirely.

The US should abandon its role as world policeman and focus only on its own interests, letting the world order itself naturally.

Final Thoughts: The Limits of Progressivism

Moldbug's central argument is that the **progressive world order is not sustainable** because it is based on **moral idealism rather than hard power.**

- History is cyclical, not progressive.
- Power determines legitimacy, not ideology.
- Moral interventionism leads to endless war.

Moldbug believes that **returning to classical international law** - where sovereignty is respected, war is fought without moralistic constraints, and governments are recognized based on their actual power - **is the shortest path to world peace.**

Part 6: The Lost Theory of Government *(May 22, 2008)*

Yarvin begins by asserting that **modern theories of government,** like those of the past (e.g., the divine right of kings), are **shaped by political power rather than objective truth** - a phenomenon he calls ***power distortion.*** He challenges the assumption that modern liberal democracy is categorically different from past regimes and suggests that its ideas persist because they serve the interests of those in power.

To redefine government from first principles, he argues that:

- **Government is a sovereign corporation** - it has control over a defined territory and functions as a single entity.

- **A good government should be evaluated by outcomes, not ideology** - a successful government is like a well-run business, judged by effectiveness, not by how its leaders are selected.
- **Centralized authority works best** - as seen in corporate management, military command, and historical governance. Divided authority leads to inefficiency and internal politics.
- **Government should be responsible** - meaning that it is accountable to a coherent group of controllers who can fire its leader if it underperforms. Yarvin proposes that government could be structured like a joint-stock company, where shares are held by those with a financial stake in good governance.
- **Profit-driven government is not inherently unethical** - contrary to democratic assumptions, private corporations provide better services than public bureaucracies. If government were structured to generate revenue (like a well-run company), it would have stronger incentives to serve its "customers" (citizens).

Yarvin acknowledges that a for-profit government raises concerns about welfare and social services but proposes an alternative: separating governance from charity. A separate entity (e.g., "Calgood") could handle social spending, allowing the government itself to focus purely on competent administration.

Finally, he introduces *secure neocameralism* - a modernized form of monarchy where technology (such as cryptographic controls) would prevent coups, making power transitions smooth and nonviolent. This structure, he argues, would eliminate the instability and dysfunction of democratic governance.

PART 7: THE UGLY TRUTH ABOUT GOVERNMENT *(MAY 29, 2008)*

Yarvin explores how modern governance evolved and why democratic politics is a façade. He argues that:

Governments disguise real power - historically, rulers have preserved the appearance of old institutions while fundamentally altering them. Just as Rome retained the Senate while shifting power to the emperor, **modern democracy maintains elections while real power rests elsewhere.**

Power hides in plain sight - it is not corporations, politicians, or conspiracies that hold true control, but an ideological system (which he later names *The Cathedral*) that manages public perception.

Democracy is an illusion - despite appearances, politicians do not actually control policy. Instead, a network of intellectuals, journalists, bureaucrats, and academics (i.e., *the Cathedral*) sets the agenda.

Public opinion is engineered - the system creates the illusion of choice while ensuring that only policies aligned with "elite" institutions (universities, media, civil service) prevail. The public is conditioned to see resistance as immoral or irrational.

The Outer Party vs. Inner Party - Yarvin compares the political system to *1984*, where the Outer Party (conservatives, Republicans) exists to create the illusion of opposition while the Inner Party (progressives, the Cathedral) actually governs. Even when right-wing figures win elections, they rarely change the system itself.

Yarvin provides historical examples:

- **McCarthy and Powell** were destroyed for challenging the system directly.
- **Reagan and Nixon** temporarily adjusted policies but ultimately failed to curb *The Cathedral's* dominance.
- **Judicial activism** (e.g., the California Supreme Court legalizing gay marriage) shows that governance operates independently of democracy, shaping laws based on elite consensus rather than public will.

He concludes by describing how the *Cathedral* adapts over time - public opinion changes only when the system is ready for it. For example, opposition to open borders is still tolerated today, but in the future, denying migrants full rights will be considered as immoral as racism.

Yarvin's ultimate question: Can this system be reformed or overthrown? He hints that answering this will require rethinking what power is and how it functions in modern governance.

Part 8: A Reset is Not a Revolution *(June 5, 2008)*

Yarvin builds on his critique of modern governance by asserting that **true power does not lie with elected officials but within *The Cathedral*** - a decentralized but unified network of elite universities and mainstream media outlets. These institutions, he argues, shape public policy and public opinion, creating an ideological monopoly without needing formal coordination.

He expands this concept to include *the Apparat* (or *Polygon*), which consists of the permanent civil service, NGOs, and other bureaucratic institutions that functionally control the state beyond electoral politics. In his view, modern governance does not operate democratically but through a *pseudoscientific* system of guided public opinion, which ensures that the ruling ideology persists regardless of election outcomes.

The Cathedral as an Evolutionary Power System

Yarvin contrasts *The Cathedral* with historical authoritarian systems, noting that it lacks a central leader or official governing body. Instead, it operates as a resilient peer-to-peer network, where institutions such as Harvard, Yale, and The New York Times act in ideological unison without explicit coordination. He compares its origins to the propaganda-heavy politics of the early 20th century, particularly FDR's New Deal, arguing that while today's *Cathedral* is less overtly a personality cult, it was born out of similar political machinations.

He critiques the foundational assumption of 20th-century governance: that government should be based on *scientific public policy*, rather than the will of elected representatives. This belief, he claims, is a form of *pseudoscience*, as it is impossible to conduct controlled experiments in governance. Because public opinion is simultaneously considered sacred and in need of elite guidance, *The Cathedral* ensures that progressivism wins both "coming and going" - when people agree with it, it is proof of correctness, and when they resist, it is proof that they need more education.

Why People Accept The Cathedral's Authority

Yarvin asks why intelligent, educated people unquestioningly trust institutions like *The New York Times* or Stanford University. He argues that this **trust is *institutional* rather than personal** - readers do not know individual journalists but assume their credibility because they speak with institutional authority (*ex cathedra*). This, he suggests, is no different from faith in religious institutions, making modern progressive governance functionally theocratic.

He argues that progressives falsely believe they are in a perpetual struggle against reactionary forces (*"The Man"*), even though they have long since won. The supposed battle against reactionary enemies, whether conservatives, corporations, or structural oppression, is a self-perpetuating myth - necessary to maintain progressivism's energy even when it dominates every major institution.

REVOLUTIONS FAIL, RESETS SUCCEED

Yarvin critiques various anti-progressive strategies:

- **Violent revolution:** Ineffective in modern democracies, as reactionary movements lack judicial or military allies.
- **Gramscian subversion (infiltrating institutions):** Unworkable because conservatives lack the unifying opportunism of progressives and are co-opted by the system.
- **Fabian incrementalism (gradual political gains):** Impossible because right-wing electoral victories never translate into real power - Republicans, for example, hold offices but do not control policy.

He argues that instead of attempting to fight progressivism through conventional means, **reactionaries should embrace a *reset*** - a total regime change that replaces the existing government with a *secure, responsible, and effective* alternative.

A *reset* is distinct from a revolution in that it is non-violent and aimed at restoring competent governance rather than seizing power for personal or ideological gain. It should happen in a single decisive action, not gradually, and must entirely replace the old regime. A failed reset risks degenerating into fascism or a new form of ideological tyranny.

The Mechanics of a Reset

Yarvin proposes that a *reset* could be achieved through an alternative electoral process:

- **Create an independent online registry of voters** willing to support regime change.
- **Once a majority is reached, form an interim administration** and demand power transfer.
- **Offer a smooth transition for the old regime**, granting amnesty and pensions to outgoing bureaucrats to minimize resistance.

He **argues that the civil service, demoralized and ineffective, would likely accept such a transition rather than fight to preserve an inefficient system.** Unlike traditional political activism, which reinforces *The Cathedral*, a reset **bypasses the existing system** entirely.

Yarvin concludes that **democracy is already dead** and that trying to restore it is pointless. Instead, reactionaries should focus on replacing the current system with a new, centralized form of government - potentially even a monarchical model, such as restoring the Stuarts in England. He suggests that what modern people lack is not democracy but competent governance, which a well-structured neocameralist system could provide.

Part 9: How to Uninstall a Cathedral (*June 12, 2008*)

Yarvin expands on his thesis that modern progressivism is an extension of Protestant Christianity, specifically a theological evolution of 19th-century liberal Protestantism. He argues that progressivism, despite its secular appearance, functions as a state religion, or what he calls an *areligion* - a belief system without gods but with its own dogmas, moral imperatives, and institutional enforcement mechanisms.

Progressivism as a Religious Continuation

Using Carlton Hayes' *History of Modern Europe* (1924), Yarvin highlights how Protestant sects gradually converged in the early 20th century, shedding explicit theological disputes in favor of a unifying moral and social vision. He suggests that modern progressives do not perceive themselves as part of a historical Christian tradition, yet their ideology operates much like a religion, imposing a moral framework that has simply been stripped of overt theological markers.

To illustrate this, Yarvin draws a **parallel between fundamentalist Christianity and modern progressivism.** He notes that while fundamentalists openly claim religious motivation, progressives see themselves as purely rational, scientific, and above ideology. However, he argues that both are inheritors of the same tradition, with progressivism functioning as a kind of atheistic Protestantism.

The Cathedral as an Established Church

Yarvin asserts that *The Cathedral* - his term for the network of elite universities and media institutions - operates as a state church in everything but name. It holds cultural hegemony, dictates moral values, and punishes dissenters. However, because it has successfully framed itself as non-religious, it evades First Amendment restrictions against government establishment of religion. This, he claims, makes it even more powerful than explicitly religious authorities.

He employs a thought experiment using *Fundamentalens*, a fictional device that swaps the positions of progressives and fundamentalists. If Harvard and Yale were run by evangelical Christians, and Bob Jones University set national policy, progressives would call this a theocracy. Since the opposite is true, he concludes that America is governed by an atheocracy - where progressivism is enforced as the *de facto* state religion.

Strategies for Removing The Cathedral

Yarvin considers two ways to dismantle The Cathedral:

- **A Soft Reset** - A legalistic, gradualist approach, in which education and media are forcibly separated from state influence, mirroring the way church and state were separated.
- **A Hard Reset** - A full regime change, dissolving The Cathedral's institutions outright and replacing them with a new governance system.

The Soft Reset (Why It Won't Work)

A soft reset would require:

- **Defunding public education** - Replacing government schools with direct tuition payments to parents, who can choose their children's education without state control.
- **Ending state recognition of academia and**

media - Just as churches do not dictate state policy, neither should universities or newspapers.
- **Eliminating credentialism** - Jobs should be based on skill-based testing rather than university degrees, reducing the power of academia to define professional legitimacy.

Yarvin argues that a soft reset is ultimately unworkable because:

The social networks that sustain The Cathedral (academics, journalists, NGOs, bureaucrats) would persist even without formal state support.

Democracy itself ensures that **those who control mass opinion will always control policy.** Even if universities lost state funding, their influence would remain intact.

A soft reset requires just as much political power as a hard reset - so why not go all the way?

THE HARD RESET (WHAT MUST BE DONE)

A hard reset means total regime change:

- **Nationalizing The Cathedral** - All media, universities, NGOs, and foundations should be forcibly liquidated. Their assets should be sold off, and their names (e.g., *The New York Times*, *Harvard*) permanently retired.
- **Immediate Replacement of the Bureaucracy** - Every government official, from elected officials to administrative clerks, should be dismissed and replaced.
- **Elimination of Ideological Influence** - Without state backing, progressive ideology would lose its

monopoly, allowing alternative viewpoints to emerge.

Yarvin compares this to historical events such as Henry VIII's dissolution of the monasteries or the suppression of the Jesuits. **The goal is not to *reform* these institutions but to *end* them, ensuring that they cannot regenerate and regain power.**

PART 10: A SIMPLE SOVEREIGN BANKRUPTCY PROCEDURE *(JUNE 19, 2008)*

Having proposed a hard reset of the U.S. government, Yarvin shifts to the mechanics of implementing regime change. He compares this process to a corporate bankruptcy, where a failing company is liquidated and restructured under new management.

THE GOVERNMENT AS A CORPORATION

Yarvin argues that the U.S. government is fundamentally a corporation - albeit one that has lost financial discipline. He proposes treating regime change as a **sovereign bankruptcy**, in which the government's debts, obligations, and governance structures are entirely restructured.

Steps of Sovereign Bankruptcy and Restoration
Appointment of a Receiver

- A transitional leader, wielding absolute authority, would take control to ensure an orderly restructuring.
- The Receiver's power would be limited to two years, after which a stable post-democratic government must be in place.

Financial Restructuring

- **Abolishing fiat currency** - Replacing the U.S. dollar (which Yarvin considers equity in a failing company) with a new stable currency backed by gold.
- **Debt liquidation** - Existing government debt should be converted into equity in a new sovereign corporation.
- **Ending entitlement spending** - Programs like Social Security and Medicare should be replaced with lump-sum payouts, eliminating future liabilities.
- **Elimination of Dysfunctional Governance**
- **Mass retirement of government employees** - Rather than simply firing them, they should be given generous severance to prevent resistance.
- **Abolition of democracy** - Democratic governance inherently leads to the rise of ideological movements like The Cathedral. Yarvin proposes replacing it with an absolute corporate-style governance model.

Restoring Law and Order

- **Ending "No-Go Zones"** - Violence and criminal subcultures (e.g., gangs) should be treated as paramilitary forces and eliminated.
- **Revitalizing cities** - Destroying brutalist architecture and restoring aesthetic urban planning would symbolically mark the end of the progressive era.

Final Transition to a New Government

- **Post-democratic sovereignty** - Instead of voting-based governance, Yarvin envisions a state run like a stable corporate monarchy, where leaders are selected based on competence rather than popular appeal.
- **Elimination of ideological control** - With The Cathedral dismantled, public opinion would no longer be manipulated to sustain the previous regime.

Conclusion: The Inevitable Fall of the Current Regime

Yarvin suggests that the **existing U.S. government is financially and ideologically bankrupt.** While a restoration may seem extreme by modern standards, he argues that such change is inevitable once enough people recognize that the current system is beyond reform.

He closes with the provocative claim that, just as past failed governments were replaced, the same fate awaits liberal democracy - and that it is only a matter of time before a sovereign bankruptcy process leads to a *hard reset* of the American state.

PART 11: THE TRUTH ABOUT LEFT AND RIGHT

Summary:

In this section, Yarvin addresses the reader as an "open-minded progressive" and revisits his provocative proposal to replace democracy with a sovereign corporation led by a Receiver. He oscillates between ironic detachment and serious argumentation, suggesting that the current democratic order is unsalvageable. The chapter explores the nature of political alignment by constructing an abstract political spectrum on an imaginary planet, Urplat, where the competing ideologies are labeled "M" and "Q."

Key Arguments:

The Problem of Political Alignment: Yarvin proposes an analytical framework in which two opposing principles, M and Q, represent fundamental contradictions. These can map onto our world's political left and right but remain undefined in their moral quality at first.

Competitiveness of Ideologies: The popularity of an idea does not determine its truth. Q is more attractive to intellectuals and spreads like a parasite through academia and media, regardless of its merit.

The Pronomian-Antinomian Divide: Yarvin introduces the concept of "pronomianism" (favoring order and formalized agreements) versus "antinomianism" (opposing structured order).

The Nomos (Structure of Promises): Pronomianism values the upholding of agreements, property rights, and hierarchical governance structures. It supports sovereignty as a corporate-like ownership model.

Antinomianism as a Revolutionary Force: Antinomianism seeks to break down traditional social structures and redistribute power. Yarvin sees libertarianism as a milder form of antinomianism and Marxism as its most extreme form, advocating destruction over order.

The Failure of Bureaucratic Democracy: Modern liberal democracy leads to bureaucratic sclerosis rather than effective governance. Instead of ensuring order, it creates inefficiency and power leakage through excessive proceduralism.

Restoration as a Radical Solution: Yarvin argues that instead of attempting to reform or conserve the system, true reactionaries must embrace a complete restoration, replacing democracy with a new form of absolute governance.

Takeaways:

- Yarvin portrays leftism (Q) as a parasitic ideological force that spreads by co-opting institutions.
- He proposes a return to rigid property rights and hierarchical order (M) as the only path to stability.
- Bureaucratic democracy weakens governance rather than strengthening it, leading to a slow decline.
- A true restoration must reject both leftist ideology and traditional conservatism, embracing a more radical restructuring of power.

PART 11: THE TRUTH ABOUT LEFT AND RIGHT

Summary:

In this section, Yarvin addresses the reader as an "open-minded progressive" and revisits his provocative proposal to replace democracy with a sovereign corporation led by a Receiver. He oscillates between ironic detachment and serious argumentation, suggesting that the current democratic order is unsalvageable. The chapter explores the nature of political alignment by constructing an abstract political spectrum on an imaginary planet, Urplat, where the competing ideologies are labeled "M" and "Q."

Key Arguments:

The Problem of Political Alignment: Yarvin proposes an analytical framework in which two opposing principles, M and Q, represent fundamental contradictions. These can map onto our world's political left and right but remain undefined in their moral quality at first.

Competitiveness of Ideologies: The popularity of an idea does not determine its truth. Q is more attractive to intellectuals and spreads like a parasite through academia and media, regardless of its merit.

The Pronomian-Antinomian Divide: Yarvin introduces the concept of "pronomianism" (favoring order and formalized agreements) versus "antinomianism" (opposing structured order).

The Nomos (Structure of Promises): Pronomianism values the upholding of agreements, property rights, and hierarchical governance structures. It supports sovereignty as a corporate-like ownership model.

Antinomianism as a Revolutionary Force: Antinomianism seeks to break down traditional social structures and redistribute power. Yarvin sees libertarianism as a milder form of antinomianism and Marxism as its most extreme form, advocating destruction over order.

The Failure of Bureaucratic Democracy: Modern liberal democracy leads to bureaucratic sclerosis rather than effective governance. Instead of ensuring order, it creates inefficiency and power leakage through excessive proceduralism.

Restoration as a Radical Solution: Yarvin argues that instead of attempting to reform or conserve the system, true reactionaries must embrace a complete restoration, replacing democracy with a new form of absolute governance.

Takeaways:

- Yarvin portrays leftism (Q) as a parasitic ideological force that spreads by co-opting institutions.
- He proposes a return to rigid property rights and hierarchical order (M) as the only path to stability.
- Bureaucratic democracy weakens governance rather than strengthening it, leading to a slow decline.

- A true restoration must reject both leftist ideology and traditional conservatism, embracing a more radical restructuring of power.

PART 12: WHAT IS TO BE DONE?

Summary:

In this section, Yarvin draws from Lenin's famous question to propose his own version of a radical political transformation. He contends that the **primary cause of suffering in the modern world is bad government,** which cannot be fixed through incremental reform. Instead, he argues for a complete replacement of democratic governance with a corporate model - what he calls "neocameralism."

Key Arguments:

The Red Pill vs. The Blue Pill: Yarvin contrasts two worldviews - one where progress is real and democracy works (the "blue pill"), and one where democracy is a decaying system camouflaged by technological progress (the "red pill"). He argues that taking the red pill reveals that modern governance has not improved but has been propped up by material advancements.

The Masking Effect of Technological Progress: Yarvin posits that without scientific and technological advancements, the failures of modern governance would be glaringly obvious. He uses historical examples to argue that 19th-century governments were more effective at rebuilding cities and maintaining order, even without modern tools.

Decaying Governance: While technology has advanced, government itself has worsened. Yarvin argues that if modern governments were stripped of their technological advantages, they would be seen as catastrophically incompetent compared to their predecessors.

Neocameralism as the Solution: The best way to ensure

effective governance is to structure the government as a corporation that seeks to maximize shareholder value. By aligning government incentives with profitability, he argues that governance would become more competent and stable.

The Role of the Receiver: Yarvin envisions a scenario in which the United States Government ("Washcorp") is liquidated and replaced by a system of sovereign corporations. A "Receiver" - analogous to a bankruptcy administrator - would take control, quelling unrest and reforming governance.

Avoiding the Mistakes of Fascism and Democracy: Yarvin acknowledges the dangers of absolute power and argues that fascism failed due to its reliance on mass politics. Instead of dictatorship, he proposes corporate governance where shareholders hold power, ensuring accountability without democratic inefficiencies.

Implementation and Transition: Since traditional democratic processes cannot be used to dismantle democracy itself, Yarvin suggests an alternative method: a transition in which governance is restructured through economic mechanisms rather than political ones. He speculates that a carefully chosen elite, such as a board of trustees made up of airline pilots, doctors, and military officers, could be entrusted with overseeing this transformation.

Takeaways:

- Yarvin argues that democracy's failures are hidden by technological progress, making it seem more effective than it really is.
- The only solution is a full replacement of democracy with neocameralism, where governance operates like a corporation.
- The transition to this new system would require a controlled process led by a trustworthy elite rather than a mass political movement.

- Neocameralism would prevent the failures of both democracy and fascism by eliminating mass political participation and structuring governance around profit-driven accountability.

PART 13: TACTICS AND STRUCTURES OF ANY PROSPECTIVE RESTORATION

Summary:

Yarvin now moves from theory to practical implementation, discussing how a democratic system could be peacefully and permanently replaced with a neocameralist order. He argues that a successful transition requires not revolution but restoration - a controlled transfer of power that minimizes disruption while maximizing legitimacy.

Key Arguments:

A Restoration, Not a Revolution: Yarvin emphasizes that neocameralism is not about violent overthrow but about transitioning power in a way that avoids chaos. He contrasts his vision with historical revolutions, which often resulted in instability and mass violence.

A Political vs. Military Coup: Yarvin outlines two possible mechanisms for transitioning away from democracy:

A military coup: Where the armed forces assume control and impose order.

A political coup (democoup): A broad-based movement that pressures the government into voluntarily dissolving itself in favor of a new system.

How a Democoup Would Work: Yarvin argues that **rather than engaging in mass electoral politics, supporters of a restoration should focus on consolidating elite opinion and applying direct pressure on existing institutions.** This involves building a movement centered on an agreed-upon goal (such as replacing democracy with a shareholder-run government) rather than promoting specific candidates or policies.

The Role of the Trust: Instead of democracy, Yarvin proposes a transitional governing body called the **Trust**, which would oversee the conversion of government assets and authority into a corporate structure. The Trust would be composed of highly qualified, responsible individuals selected not by election but through a pre-established heuristic test.

The Pilot Heuristic Test: One of Yarvin's most controversial suggestions is that the **Trustees** should be selected based on a specific criterion - such as being a certified pilot, doctor, or military officer. He argues that these professions demand responsibility and competence, making them ideal candidates for guiding the transition.

Takeaways:

- Yarvin insists that neocameralism must be achieved through peaceful, structured transition rather than violence.
- A democoup, rather than an electoral movement, is the best way to dissolve democracy.
- A small, competent elite should oversee the transition rather than relying on mass participation.
- The **Trust** would serve as the transitional authority, ensuring continuity and legitimacy.

Part 14: Rules for Reactionaries

Summary:

In this concluding section of the series, Yarvin directly addresses his "open-minded progressive" readers, asserting that they have now advanced beyond conventional democratic assumptions and are prepared to grasp the necessity of dismantling the existing political order. He articulates what he sees as the fundamental problems with democracy, explores the mechanics of how it perpetuates itself, and proposes a set of guiding principles for reactionaries who seek to replace it. The section is characterized by Yarvin's signature mix of irony, dodgy historical analysis, and polemical intensity.

Key Arguments:

Democracy is a Self-Destructive System: Yarvin reiterates that democracy inherently degenerates into factional warfare, where power is sought not for governance but for self-enrichment. He draws from historical figures like Noah Webster to illustrate how political factions inevitably prioritize their own survival over the public good.

The Cathedral and the Re-Education of the Masses: According to Yarvin, democratic systems "elect a new people" not just through mass immigration but through the ideological capture of education, media, and academia - what he calls "the Cathedral." This feedback loop ensures that democracy perpetuates itself by controlling information and suppressing dissent.

Libertarians Are Naïve: Yarvin critiques libertarians for believing they can reform democracy into a system that protects individual liberties. He argues that libertarian democracy is a contradiction in terms, as democracy incentivizes the expansion of state power rather than its reduction.

The Failure of Modern Governance: Yarvin contrasts 19th-century governments, which he claims were more competent despite having fewer technological advantages, with modern democratic bureaucracies, which he views as inefficient and corrupt.

The Need for a 'Reset' Rather than Reform: Yarvin insists that piecemeal reforms are futile. Instead, he advocates for a total rejection of democratic governance in favor of a more stable, hierarchical alternative. He presents various possible replacements, including military rule, corporate governance, and restricted suffrage based on property ownership.

Political Power Cannot Be Won through Normal Electoral Means: Yarvin argues that restoration cannot be achieved by defeating the left or right in conventional elections. Instead, the system must be delegitimized entirely, much like communism was delegitimized before its collapse.

The Only Weapon Is Truth: Yarvin asserts that reactionaries must avoid deceit and rely solely on exposing the failures and contradictions of democracy. He proposes an intellectual strategy modeled on websites like Climate Audit and Gene Expression, which challenge academic orthodoxies by exposing their weaknesses.

Building a Counter-Cathedral: Yarvin suggests creating an alternative intellectual network that systematically dismantles the assumptions of modern democratic governance. This "Resartus" movement would serve as a counterweight to the current ideological hegemony of universities and media.

Quality over Quantity in Building a Movement: Yarvin argues that early reactionary efforts should focus on attracting a small, intellectually elite group rather than amassing popular support. He sees this as a long-term strategy for undermining the legitimacy of the current system.

Takeaways:

- Democracy inevitably degrades into factionalism and self-perpetuating bureaucratic decay.
- The modern electorate is shaped by media and education institutions that reinforce the system's legitimacy, making reform impossible.
- Libertarians fail to recognize that democracy structurally opposes their goals of minimal government.

- The only path forward is a full rejection of democratic governance and the construction of an alternative intellectual framework to undermine it.
- Reactionaries should focus on quality over quantity, building a highly competent network before engaging in mass movements.

CONCLUSION: THE NEOREACTIONARY THESIS IN FULL

Curtis Yarvin's 14-part series lays out a fundamental critique of modern governance, democracy, and the ideological structures that sustain them. Over the course of these essays, he builds a case for why liberal democracy - far from being the pinnacle of political development - is an unstable and self-perpetuating system that erodes effective governance, rewards mediocrity, and entrenches ideological control. His argument is radical but *internally* coherent, drawing on incomplete historical analogies, political theory, and an engineering mindset to propose a drastic alternative: a structured, corporate-style sovereign state that eliminates the inefficiencies and dysfunction of democratic rule.

The Core Critiques of Democracy

Yarvin's primary argument is that democracy is not a stable or self-correcting system but an accelerating feedback loop that incentivizes short-term political struggles rather than long-term governance. He presents two core failures of democracy:

First-Order Problem: Political factions will always seek to maximize their power and influence at the expense of the system's long-term stability, leading to internal strife, mismanagement, and ideological capture.

Second-Order Problem: Democracy inevitably reshapes its population and cultural environment to ensure its continued dominance - what he calls the government "electing a new people." Through media, academia ("the Cathedral"), and bureaucratic structures, democracy maintains its grip not through explicit coercion but through ideological reinforcement.

The result is a system that decays over time, shifting further into ideological control while failing to deliver competent governance. Instead of a system that selects for excellence, democracy selects for those who are best at navigating its incentives - career politicians, bureaucrats, and academics who reinforce the ruling ideology.

The Proposed Alternative: Sovereign Corporations

Yarvin's solution is a radical departure from democratic traditions. He envisions a government structured like a corporation, where sovereign power is centralized, governance is profit-driven, and the administration is insulated from the short-term political struggles that define democracies. His model, often referred to as "neocameralism," suggests:

A Government-Owned by Shareholders: Sovereignty should be treated like private property, where governance operates as a rational enterprise with clear incentives aligned toward long-term stability and prosperity.

Elimination of Mass Political Participation: Yarvin dismisses democratic decision-making as inherently flawed and corruptible, advocating for a governance structure that removes mass electoral politics entirely.

Rule by a Competent Elite: Instead of democratic elections, governance should be entrusted to an elite managerial class whose decisions are guided by maximizing the health and stability of the state.

The Role of Ideology and the Cathedral

A recurring theme in Yarvin's work is his critique of the "Cathedral" - his term for the intertwined influence of academia, media, and bureaucracy in shaping mass opinion. He argues that this structure serves as an ideological control mechanism, maintaining the dominance of progressive values and ensuring that political opposition is effectively marginalized. Unlike traditional authoritarian propaganda, the Cathedral does not rely on direct coercion but on the self-reinforcing nature of institutions that claim moral and intellectual authority.

The key insight here is that democracy does not merely reflect the will of the people but actively shapes it. Through education, media narratives, and social norms, democratic societies generate ideological compliance, making meaningful opposition increasingly difficult. Yarvin frames this as a systemic issue rather than a conspiracy, emphasizing that the incentives of democracy naturally produce this outcome over time.

The Path to Restoration

Yarvin offers a series of "Rules for Reactionaries" to guide those who reject the current order and seek an alternative. These rules emphasize:

A Clean Break from the Past: He argues that attempting to reform democracy from within is futile. A complete reset - a "restoration" - is required.

Rejection of Partisan Struggles: The traditional left-right divide is meaningless within a fundamentally broken system. Instead of conservative reform or progressive expansion, Yarvin calls for a total rejection of the framework itself.

Truth as the Primary Weapon: Since mass politics is off the table, Yarvin suggests that the only effective means of challenging the system is through rigorous intellectual opposition - exposing contradictions, dismantling ideological assumptions, and building alternative narratives.

His vision of transition is less clear. While he acknowledges that a direct seizure of power is unrealistic, he speculates about a gradual shift through elite buy-in, technological disruption, or a collapse of democratic institutions that necessitates a new form of governance.

Final Assessment: The Limits and Implications of Yarvin's Vision

Yarvin's work is provocative and deeply critical of the existing order, but it raises several important questions:

Is his historical analysis selective? While he identifies real flaws in democracy, his portrayal of historical alternatives often downplays their own structural failures.

Can a sovereign corporation truly be stable? While neocameralism offers a clean theoretical model, it assumes that shareholders or managers will act with long-term incentives rather than seeking immediate power and profit - an assumption that history does not necessarily support.

What about individual rights and liberties? Yarvin's model dismisses democracy's failures but does not fully address how a corporate-run government would protect individual freedoms beyond mere efficiency.

Despite these critiques, his work provides a valuable counterpoint to mainstream political thought. By questioning democracy's inevitability and exposing its hidden failures, he forces readers to reconsider foundational political assumptions. Whether one agrees with his solutions or not, Yarvin's critique remains one of the most radical and unflinching reassessments of modern governance in the 21st century.

Closing Thought: The Challenge of the Reactionary Vision

If Yarvin's thesis is to be believed, then the modern world is engaged in a long, slow-motion collapse into bureaucratic stagnation and ideological conformity. His solution - replacing democracy with a sovereign corporation - offers a stark alternative, one that reimagines governance as a structured, hierarchical enterprise rather than a chaotic, majoritarian process. Yet, for all its logic, his vision remains largely theoretical, with no clear path from the present order to his proposed future.

Ultimately, the core challenge of Yarvin's neoreactionary vision is not whether it is intellectually coherent, but whether it is feasible. History has not yet provided a definitive test of his ideas, but the failures of democracy that he outlines remain a persistent challenge for any modern political system. As long as those failures continue, his critique will remain relevant - and his vision, however radical, will continue to provoke debate.

Connect the Dots

Consider these questions:

- Why does Moldbug compare progressivism to a religious belief system?
- How does institutional trust shape people's understanding of history and politics?
- What are the contradictions Moldbug identifies in progressive narratives?
- How does power sustain itself through moral authority rather than force?

Pick three examples from the world around you. For each, analyze:

- Who decides what is considered true or false?
- How do institutions shape public perception?
- Are there contradictions in the dominant narrative?

Some examples to consider:

- **News and journalism** (How do certain events get framed? What topics are treated as unquestionable?)
- **History education** (What parts of history are emphasized or ignored? Who writes the textbooks?)
- **Social movements** (How are some nationalist or revolutionary movements celebrated while others are condemned?)
- **Political institutions** (How does moral legitimacy influence global politics? Who gets to define what is "just" intervention?)
- **Online censorship and discourse** (Who decides what speech is acceptable? How do platforms enforce ideological conformity?)

Do you agree with Moldbug that progressivism operates as a self-reinforcing belief system? Why or why not? If institutional narratives are shaped by power, what does that mean for the pursuit of truth?

"The Dark Enlightenment" by Nick Land

Land's Vision of Democratic Doom

Nick Land's *The Dark Enlightenment* systematically dismantles modern democracy, progressing from political critique to racial analysis and ultimately to technological prophecy. Unlike traditional conservative critiques that seek to slow progressive change, Land argues that **democracy is not just flawed but inherently self-destructive. Reform is impossible; the only viable response is total rejection.**

Democracy's Inherent Corruption

Land's argument begins with democracy's structural flaws. He asserts that **democratic governance creates perverse incentives:** politicians secure power by bribing the electorate with social programs and government spending. Since their terms are temporary, they prioritize short-term popularity over long-term stability. The inevitable result is an ever-expanding state that consumes society's productive capacity.

But to Land, this is not just poor governance - it is democracy's core design. He cites Peter Thiel's 2009 declaration that "freedom and democracy are incompatible" as a foundational principle. The system rewards irresponsibility and punishes discipline, accelerating civilizational decline.

Democracy as a One-Way Process

Land emphasizes that democracy, once expanded, cannot be undone. Universal suffrage and mass participation create a ratchet effect, making it impossible to return to aristocratic, hierarchical rule. He argues that conservative attempts to slow or reverse progressive reforms are doomed because democracy's internal logic always pushes toward greater inclusivity, economic redistribution, and bureaucratic expansion - leading ultimately to collapse.

The Cathedral: Democracy as a Religious System

Land deepens his critique by arguing that democracy is sustained not just by political structures but by an ideological apparatus he calls *the Cathedral*. Borrowing from Mencius Moldbug, he describes the Cathedral as a network of universities, media institutions, and bureaucracies that enforce progressive orthodoxy. Unlike traditional censorship, **the Cathedral does not merely suppress dissent - it renders alternative ideas *unthinkable*.**

Under this system, any resistance to progressive ideals is framed as evidence of moral failure, justifying ever-greater interventions. The Cathedral does not govern democratically - it governs *the democratic mind*, ensuring that ideological opponents are either assimilated or discredited.

RACE AS DEMOCRACY'S FATAL CONTRADICTION

At the heart of democracy's instability, Land argues, lies racial politics. In diverse societies, democracy inevitably devolves into tribal warfare, as different groups compete for state resources. **The Cathedral, rather than mitigating this conflict, *requires* permanent racial grievance** to justify its expansion. If racial inequality were ever "solved," the entire progressive project would lose its moral foundation.

This dynamic is most visible in urban geography. Land examines the "core-crashed donut" pattern of American cities, where prosperous suburbs surround decaying centers. He interprets "white flight" not simply as economic migration or racism but as *slow-motion secession* - a spontaneous attempt to escape democracy's contradictions. Even progressive elites who advocate for integration choose segregation in practice, proving the inescapable nature of tribal politics.

THE AMERICAN CIVIL WAR AND CROSS-CODED HISTORY

Land sees the American Civil War as a pivotal moment that solidified democracy's control. By framing the conflict as a struggle between emancipation and independence, the Cathedral ensured that any future resistance to central authority could be coded as racist. This "cross-coded" history ensures that every political question is reframed through a moral lens that justifies state expansion.

This analysis leads Land to reject both mainstream conservatism and white nationalism.

- **Conservatives** fail because they remain trapped in the Cathedral's moral framework. Any opposition

to progressive policy is automatically labeled racist, forcing conservatives into defensive posturing.
- **White nationalists** fail because Western civilization's strength historically came from suppressing tribal instincts in favor of abstract institutions. Land argues that Europeans, due to unique historical patterns of "outbreeding," are particularly ill-suited for ethnic identity politics.

Cybernetics, Capital, and the Inevitability of Collapse

Land introduces cybernetics - the study of systems, feedback loops, and self-regulation - to explain why democracy is not just unstable but doomed. He distinguishes between:

- **Positive feedback loops** – runaway cycles that accelerate instability (e.g., democratic expansion, progressive ideology, mass political participation).
- **Negative feedback loops** – self-correcting mechanisms that maintain equilibrium (e.g., free markets, AI-driven capitalism).

He argues that d**emocracy functions as a *positive feedback loop* that leads to its own destruction**: each new reform requires further expansion, each new crisis justifies more government intervention. In contrast, **techno-commercial capitalism, left to its own devices, would operate as a *negative feedback loop*,** self-regulating through market forces and technological efficiency.

Exit: Land's Solution to Democratic Collapse

Since democracy cannot be salvaged and neither conservatism nor racial nationalism offer viable alternatives, Land advocates for *exit* - a complete abandonment of democratic institutions. This takes multiple forms:

- **Political Exit:** Seasteading, charter cities, and alternative governance models.
- **Economic Exit:** Cryptocurrency and parallel markets independent of state control.
- **Cultural Exit:** Private communities and digital enclaves that detach from mainstream society.
- **Biological Exit:** Genetic engineering and human enhancement to transcend current limitations.

For Land, the endgame of *The Dark Enlightenment* is not just a political shift but a fundamental transformation of what it means to be human.

Beyond Human Politics: Accelerationism and the Bionic Horizon

Land does not simply argue that democracy is unsustainable - he argues that its collapse should be welcomed and accelerated. In his framework, political decay is not something to resist but something to *push forward*, hastening the inevitable implosion of failing institutions. This is the core of ***accelerationism*: rather than attempting to salvage democracy, neo-reactionaries should drive it to its logical endpoint,** allowing superior systems to emerge from the wreckage.

Land believes that the Cathedral is not just enforcing progressive orthodoxy but actively guiding civilization toward self-destruction. By maintaining an unsustainable ideological and economic order, it ensures that society remains in a state of managed decline. But this decline will not last indefinitely - eventually, demographic pressures, economic collapse, and technological shifts will make governance through ideological coercion impossible. At that point, new, post-democratic power structures will take control.

This transition is not a question of *if* but *when*. Land offers three possible futures:

1. **Modernity 2.0** – A new center of global power (likely China) rises, freed from Western democratic decay.
2. **Postmodernity** – Civilizational collapse leads to a new dark age, where Malthusian limits brutally reassert themselves.
3. **Western Renaissance** – A "hard reboot" occurs through crisis and disintegration, potentially leading to new political and economic systems better adapted to reality.

THE BIONIC HORIZON: ESCAPE THROUGH TECHNOLOGY

Land does not believe that the future will simply be a repeat of past cycles of rise and fall. Instead, he argues that the most likely outcome is *technological secession* - the creation of post-human intelligence that will leave behind outdated political and biological constraints.

Here, he draws on biologist John H. Campbell's work on human evolution, envisioning *Homo autocatalyticus* - a self-modifying, technologically enhanced species that no longer relies on traditional human governance.

At this stage, the real divide is no longer left vs. right, or even human vs. machine, but between those who remain trapped in democratic decay and those who embrace technological transformation. Land refers to this process as *speciation* - the emergence of a new, post-human elite that will ultimately render current political struggles meaningless.

Conclusion: The Dark Enlightenment as Technological Secession

The Dark Enlightenment presents a radical alternative to both democratic progressivism and conservative nostalgia. Land's vision begins as a critique of democracy, expands into an analysis of race and history, and ultimately resolves in a call for technological transcendence. His final prediction is stark: while most of society remains trapped in the slow-motion collapse of democracy, a new technological elite is already preparing for what he calls *speciation* - the emergence of a genuinely post-human future.

Connect the Dots

Consider these questions:

- Why does Land believe democracy is doomed to fail?
- How does the Cathedral shape public opinion? Can you think of real-world examples?
- What makes accelerationism different from just wanting political change?
- If democracy is collapsing, what comes next?
- Pick three examples from the world around you. For each, analyze:
- How power is being used or maintained
- Whether resistance is possible or futile

- Whether technology is changing how decisions are made

Some examples to consider:

- **News and social media** (Who decides what information gets amplified? Who is "allowed" to speak?)
- **Politics and government** (Do politicians focus on long-term solutions or short-term popularity?)
- **Technology and AI** (Are machines and algorithms already making decisions that humans used to make?)
- **Where people live** (Why do cities change over time? What causes people to move away?)
- **Education and universities** (Who decides what ideas are acceptable to discuss in a classroom?)

Do you agree with Land that democracy is an unsustainable system? Why or why not? If democracy fails, what do you think would replace it?

"Reactionary Philosophy in a... Nutshell"

R*eactionary Philosophy in an Enormous, Planet-Sized Nutshell* by Scott Alexander (March 3, 2013)

Introduction: Why Summarize Reactionary Thought?

Scott Alexander sets out to provide a summary of reactionary ideas, responding to the claim that their worldview is too complex for easy explanation. While acknowledging that reactionary arguments often rely on intuition and historical analogies rather than formal logic, he aims to present them fairly before critiquing them. His central question: ***Is modern society truly better than its predecessors, or is that just an assumption?***

The Suspicion of Progress: Is Our Era Truly Special?

Every civilization considers itself the pinnacle of human achievement - Imperial China, medieval Spain, Soviet Russia.

But history shows that societies are often blind to their own flaws. If we recognize this pattern, should we assume that 21st-century liberal democracy has finally perfected governance? Progressives argue that free speech and open institutions ensure continued improvement, while reactionaries challenge this assumption.

The Progressive Immune System: Why Certain Ideas Are Untouchable

Alexander introduces the idea that modern **liberal democracy suppresses dissent much like older regimes** - just in a subtler way. Instead of executing heretics or exiling dissidents, today's progressives create social taboos that make certain ideas (e.g., rolling back civil rights laws) unthinkable. Those who propose reversing progressive changes face ostracization, career destruction, or violence. Reactionaries argue that this functions as an ideological immune system, shielding progressivism from challenges.

The Leftward Drift: Why Society Moves in Only One Direction

Liberal democracy allows critique - but only within a narrow range. Advocating for even more progressive policies is praised as bold and forward-thinking, but suggesting a reversal of recent reforms (e.g., repealing women's suffrage) is met with outrage. Since at least the 18th century, Western politics has moved consistently leftward, from monarchy to democracy, from traditionalist values to increasing progressivism. Reactionaries argue this drift is neither inevitable nor necessarily beneficial.

The Information Problem: Can We Trust Modern Institutions?

Reactionaries contend that academia, media, and mainstream discourse are biased toward progressivism. Alexander points to sociology as an example: universities claim neutrality but are dominated by scholars who view their role as advancing social justice. Just as past scientific consensus justified racism, modern academia might be producing politically convenient but flawed conclusions. Reactionaries argue that their ideas are not absent because they are wrong, but because they are suppressed.

Are We Actually Better Off? Or Just More Technologically Advanced?

Many modern improvements - wealth, medicine, life expectancy - are due to technological advances rather than governance or cultural progress. If today's political and social systems are inherently superior, we should see improvements in areas that technology doesn't directly affect, such as crime rates, education quality, and social cohesion. Reactionaries argue that in many of these areas, we have regressed.

The Illusion of Safety: Were the Past and Present Actually Different?

Mencius Moldbug argues that despite modern policing, CCTV, and forensic advancements, 21st-century cities are often more dangerous than their 19th-century counterparts. Victorian England, for example, had lower violent crime rates despite lacking modern law enforcement tools. If safety were purely a function of technology, crime should have declined. Reactionaries argue that cultural and political changes - such as progressive policies and weakened law enforcement - are to blame.

EDUCATION: ARE WE ACTUALLY SMARTER?

Modern society takes pride in mass education, but reactionaries argue that past elites were far more knowledgeable than today's intellectual class. Alexander highlights the 1899 Harvard entrance exam, which required Latin, Greek, and advanced mathematics - subjects rarely mastered by modern students. He also notes that early U.S. presidents were often multilingual, whereas recent ones struggle with basic foreign language skills. If we truly lived in an era of intellectual progress, why does our leadership class seem less educated?

PROGRESS IN MORALITY: IS SOCIETY MORE TOLERANT AND HUMANE?

Liberal democracy celebrates progress in race, gender, and human rights as moral advancement. Reactionaries challenge this claim, offering three explanations for group disparities:

- **Externalists**: Structural oppression (e.g., colonialism, systemic racism) causes inequality.
- **Culturalists**: Traditions and social norms shape outcomes.
- **Biologicalists**: Genetic differences influence societal success (Alexander distances himself from this view).

Alexander notes that some historically oppressed groups - such as Jews and Asians - outperform the general population, while others do not. If discrimination were the sole explanation for disparities, why do different groups respond differently to oppression?

The Culturalist Perspective: Why Some Groups Succeed

Reactionaries argue that culture, rather than oppression, explains long-term group differences. The success of Jewish and Chinese immigrants - despite initial discrimination - suggests that assimilation-friendly values drive prosperity. Policies that discourage assimilation (e.g., multiculturalism, bilingual education) may prevent struggling groups from adopting more successful norms. Alexander contrasts this with past immigration waves, where Irish and Italian immigrants integrated more successfully than some modern immigrant groups.

Immigration: The Risks of Importing Cultural Clashes

If culture matters more than oppression, then large-scale immigration from societies with vastly different values could destabilize Western countries. Reactionaries argue that importing millions of people from authoritarian, patriarchal, or violent cultures risks eroding liberal norms. Historical U.S. immigration policies (e.g., the 1924 Immigration Act) favored assimilation-friendly groups, while modern policies focus on non-discrimination without considering long-term cultural effects.

Alexander offers a thought experiment:

- Imagine a utopian, eco-friendly progressive society.

- Now, suppose millions of Americans - with their guns, fast food, and religious conservatism - moved in.
- Over time, this utopia would start looking like America.

He applies this logic to real-world immigration, arguing that **mass migration from authoritarian, patriarchal, or violent cultures** could erode Western liberal norms.

The Uncanny Valley of Dictatorship: When Half-Measures Make Everything Worse

Reactionaries argue that the worst form of government is not full democracy or full dictatorship but something in between - **a state where rulers lack both legitimacy and absolute power.** Alexander describes this as the "uncanny valley" of dictatorship: a government that is authoritarian enough to suppress dissent but too weak to establish long-term stability.

A truly strong dictatorship, in this view, does not constantly need to repress its citizens because it has already cemented its authority. By contrast, u**nstable dictatorships - where leaders are uncertain of their control - resort to unpredictable crackdowns,** creating more suffering than if they had total dominance from the outset.

Case Study: Colonial vs. Post-Colonial Rule

British and French colonial administrations maintained relative stability through overwhelming power and decisive governance.

In contrast, many post-colonial governments inherited Western legal structures but lacked the authority to govern effectively. This led to prolonged civil conflicts, weak enforcement, and cycles of coups.

Moldbug's *Fnargl* thought experiment aims to illustrate this idea: If an invincible dictator existed, he would have no need to suppress free speech, impose arbitrary laws, or eliminate rivals - because his power would never be threatened. Paradoxically, a dictator with total control may create a more stable and predictable society than one who must constantly fight for legitimacy.

Alexander applies this argument to criminal justice, comparing modern prison systems with historical corporal punishment.

Modern punishment: A convict today may spend years in prison, enduring violence and psychological trauma, while becoming unemployable.

Historical punishment: A whipping (as used in past legal systems) was painful but brief, allowing criminals to reintegrate into society quickly.

Reactionaries argue that progressive opposition to corporal punishment has led to a cruel and inefficient middle ground - where punishments are long and ineffective rather than immediate and decisive.

Modern Warfare: Why Being "Humanitarian" Makes Wars Worse

Reactionaries argue that modern "humanitarian" warfare prolongs suffering rather than reducing it. Before the mid-20th century, wars were often brutal but decisive, leading to swift resolutions. Today, restrictions on warfare - such as rules of engagement, proportional response, and concerns about civilian casualties - result in conflicts that drag on indefinitely.

Comparison: Decisive vs. Prolonged Warfare

- **Decisive war:** In the colonial era, Britain and France would quickly pacify a rebellious territory through overwhelming force, preventing drawn-out resistance.

- **Prolonged war:** Modern conflicts (e.g., Iraq, Vietnam, Afghanistan) last for decades because Western nations refuse to use full military strength.

Reactionaries argue that the Geneva Conventions and progressive moral norms have turned warfare into an "uncanny valley" - too brutal to be peaceful, but too restrained to be effective. The result:

- Endless insurgencies instead of clear victories.
- Civilian casualties increasing due to prolonged conflict.
- Warlords and extremists exploiting Western reluctance to engage in total war.

Alexander contrasts the atomic bombings of Hiroshima and Nagasaki - which ended WWII almost immediately - with drawn-out wars like Vietnam and Iraq, which caused mass suffering over decades. The reactionary view is that if a war must be fought, it should be swift and overwhelming rather than politically constrained and indefinitely prolonged.

Connect the Dots

Consider these questions:

- Why do reactionaries believe progress is an illusion?
- How does the “progressive immune system” enforce social taboos?

- What are examples of modern issues that reactionaries claim technology hides rather than solves?
- Does history show a consistent leftward drift, or is this an oversimplification?

Pick three examples from the world around you. For each, analyze:

- How has the dominant political or cultural view changed over time?
- What forces push ideas forward or suppress alternative perspectives?
- Are these changes driven by truth, power, or historical accident?

Some examples to consider:

- **Crime and policing** (Are cities actually safer today, or do modern policies just make crime harder to report and track?)
- **Education** (Are people actually better educated today, or has the quality of knowledge declined?)
- **Media and censorship** (Are controversial views suppressed for being false or simply for being inconvenient?)
- **Gender and happiness** (Are modern social norms actually improving people's lives, or do traditional roles produce better outcomes?)
- **Immigration and cultural assimilation** (Do different groups integrate equally, or does culture affect long-term success?)

Do you think reactionaries are right to doubt the idea of progress, or is their skepticism misplaced? If society is always moving forward, how can we tell if we're heading in the right direction?

"Taking the Red Pill" by Bryce Laliberte

Taking the Red Pill: How to Look at the World Like a Neoreactionary by Bryce Laliberte (2013)

Part 1 – The Neoreactionary Mindset

Laliberte introduces neoreaction (NRx) as a fundamentally different way of viewing the world, likening it to taking the "red pill" from *The Matrix* - a metaphor for awakening from the illusions of modernity. He argues that **most people are so deeply immersed in progressive ideology that they do not even recognize it,** much like a fish is unaware of water. According to him, neoreactionaries break free from this conditioning through a dialectical process of unlearning progressive assumptions.

Modernity, he claims, enforces an artificial political consensus by suppressing genuine intellectual diversity, confining thought within a narrow, socially acceptable range. He challenges foundational modern ideas such as democracy, meritocracy, and equality, arguing that they are as arbitrary and socially constructed as monarchy, patriarchy, and religious authority were in past eras. The core neoreactionary insight, according to Laliberte, is that **human differences - biological, racial, and class-based - are real** and should be acknowledged in governance and policy rather than ignored in pursuit of a false egalitarian ideal.

Part 2 – Persuasion and Thought Reform

Laliberte contends that neoreaction is not a political ideology in the conventional sense but rather a meta-ideology - a way of analyzing the fundamental assumptions underlying all political philosophies. He describes it as a method for deconstructing progressive dogma and revealing its hidden costs.

He acknowledges that neoreactionary ideas are difficult for those steeped in modernist thought to accept but argues that persuasion is a slow process of self-examination. He critiques progressive arguments as relying heavily on emotional appeals and moral coercion rather than empirical evidence and rigorous logic.

Central to his argument is **human biodiversity (HBD)** - the controversial idea that genetic differences between individuals and groups shape intelligence, behavior, and social outcomes. He claims that progressives ignore or suppress scientific findings that contradict their belief in racial and gender equality, likening their ideology to a religious faith.

He introduces the concept of **bias**, arguing that while "midwits" (people of average intelligence) view bias as inherently bad, more intelligent individuals recognize that biases evolved for adaptive reasons. For instance, he reframes racism not as an irrational prejudice but as an evolved survival mechanism - an instinct to favor one's own group in tribal competition. Rather than eliminating biases, he suggests refining them.

PART 3 – THE NEOREACTIONARY AS AN ENEMY OF PROGRESS

Laliberte argues that **progressives view reactionaries as heretical enemies** because they reject the moral framework of progressivism. He claims that progressives believe in a utopian vision of history in which dissenters are obstacles to be re-educated, ostracized, or eliminated.

He provocatively suggests that, if progressives were truly consistent, they would logically advocate for the physical elimination of ideological opponents to expedite social progress - though he acknowledges they stop short of this due to moral and social constraints.

Neoreactionaries, he asserts, embrace their role as villains within the progressive narrative and actively oppose modernity. Rather than simply resisting progress, they seek to hijack history and steer civilization in a different direction - one that prioritizes hierarchy, stability, and realism over utopian social engineering.

PART 4 – DECLINING BIRTH RATES AND THE BREAKDOWN OF CIVILIZATION

Laliberte presents **declining birth rates as the ultimate indictment of modernity**. He argues that contemporary social norms discourage family formation, leading to demographic collapse.

He identifies three key factors:

1. **Feminism** – Encourages women to prioritize careers over motherhood, leading to lower fertility rates.
2. **Careerism** – Both men and women are pressured

to achieve economic success before starting families.

3. **The Cult of Childhood** – Modern society prolongs adolescence, emphasizing education and leisure rather than early marriage and reproduction.

He suggests that historical societies were structured to prioritize family formation, with early marriage and economic contribution beginning at younger ages. He criticizes modern policies that make raising children prohibitively expensive and argues that allowing children to work earlier would **restore healthier social structures** and incentivize large families.

His core argument is that **civilizations that fail to reproduce themselves inevitably decline and are replaced by more fertile populations** - whether through internal demographic shifts or external migration.

Part 5 – Political Philosophy and Governance

Laliberte argues that neoreaction **rejects both libertarianism and socialism** because both assume that all people are equal. Instead, he proposes a model of governance that is adapted to the unique qualities of each population rather than imposed universally.

He makes the case that **democracy only functions in small, homogeneous societies**. In large, diverse states, it leads to factionalism and dysfunction, as groups vote for benefits at the expense of others rather than prioritizing the long-term stability of the nation. He contrasts democracy with **monarchy**, which he argues is **more stable** because the ruler's personal interests are aligned with the long-term prosperity of the state.

He also **critiques modern economics for treating GDP growth as the sole measure of success**, arguing that societies should instead be judged by their ability to sustain civilization over generations. He **rejects universalism**, instead advocating a hierarchical approach where different societies adopt governance systems suited to their particular characteristics.

Part 6 – The Limits of Social Engineering

Laliberte critiques the progressive belief that social structures can be endlessly reengineered to create ideal outcomes. He argues that many social behaviors - such as **bias, tribalism, and hierarchy - are deeply embedded in human nature** and cannot simply be eliminated through policy.

He reframes **prejudice as an evolved psychological mechanism**, claiming that while it can be misapplied, it serves an adaptive purpose. He suggests that progressive attempts to "reprogram" human nature ignore biological realities and are doomed to failure.

He introduces the "God of Biomechanics", a metaphor for evolution's role in shaping human instincts. Societies, he argues, should work with human nature rather than attempting to override it.

Part 7 – The Problem of Civilization and Natural Slavery

Laliberte explores the idea that **dependence is an unavoidable part of human society**, arguing that all social structures involve some form of hierarchical control. He describes taxation, governance, and cultural obligations as **forms of "soft slavery"** in which individuals are bound by duties and dependencies.

He critiques democracy as an unstable system that prioritizes short-term individual interests over long-term civilizational stability. He draws historical parallels, arguing that past civilizations - like Rome - **collapsed due to similar forces of egalitarianism, declining birth rates, and political instability**.

His final argument is that neoreaction is fundamentally a rejection of modernity's core assumptions. Rather than seeking to reshape human nature to fit egalitarian ideals, neoreaction seeks to **design systems that align with natural human differences**.

Final Thoughts on *Taking the Red Pill*

Laliberte's series presents neoreaction as a radical rejection of democracy, egalitarianism, and progressivism in favor of **hierarchy, realism, and civilizational stability**. He **frames modernity as an unsustainable ideology** that ignores human nature, leading to dysfunction and eventual decline.

His approach blends:

- **Social Darwinism** – The belief that societies should be structured around natural selection rather than social engineering.
- **Critiques of progressive moral assumptions** – Particularly around race, gender, and equality.
- **Advocacy for alternative governance structures** – Monarchy, elite rule, and tailored systems of government.

While **highly polemical**, the series articulates the intellectual foundations of neoreaction, making it a useful resource for understanding the movement's worldview.

Connect the Dots

Consider these questions:

- What assumptions about democracy does Laliberte challenge?
- How does neoreaction define "progress" differently from mainstream thought?
- What real-world examples align with his critiques of modernity?
- If social engineering has limits, what are its most successful and least successful applications?

Pick three historical or contemporary cases and analyze:

- How modern policies either reinforce or contradict neoreactionary ideas.
- Whether alternative governance models could produce better outcomes.
- The extent to which progress is real vs. an illusion.

Here are five historical or contemporary cases you could analyze through a neoreactionary lens, considering Laliberte's critiques of democracy, progressivism, and social engineering:

- The Fall of the Roman Republic and Rise of the Roman Empire
- The Soviet Union and the Collapse of Communism
- Post-Colonial Africa and the "Failed State" Problem
- The U.S. Immigration Debate and the Question of Assimilation
- The Decline of Birth Rates in Developed Nations

"Post-Modernism's Final Causes..." by iParallax

"P*ost-Modernism's Final Causes and Pyrrhic Victory*" by iParallax (2013)

This series of essays critiques post-modernism through the lens of Aristotle's Four Causes (Material, Formal, Efficient, and Final) to explain its origins, functions, and ultimate self-destruction. The author argues that **post-modernism is an ideological parasite that thrives on prosperity, detachment from material reality, and the suppression of dissent** - yet it inevitably consumes itself by dismantling the very structures that sustain it.

Part I: Post-Modernism Through Aristotle's Four Causes *(December 12, 2013)*

Material Cause – Prosperity as a Catalyst for Post-Modernism

Post-modernism emerged in societies that no longer struggle for basic survival. Unlike past civilizations that had to maintain order, modern societies enjoy unprecedented wealth, leading people to assume stability and abundance are the natural state of things.

- **The Hidden Cost of Wealth** – Modern prosperity **insulates people from scarcity,** leading to policies that ignore trade-offs and long-term sustainability.
- **Comfort Breeds Utopian Thinking** – Societies no longer accustomed to existential threats become obsessed with **idealism over pragmatism.**

Formal Causes – The Conceptual Errors of Post-Modernism

Post-modernist thinking is structured around **three major conceptual misunderstandings:**

1. **Inability to Understand Cost** – People assume progress happens automatically rather than through sustained effort.
2. **Inability to Understand Entropy** – They ignore the fact that **civilization is inherently unnatural** and must be constantly maintained.
3. **Denial of Consequences** – Modern ideologies promote redistribution, social change, and radical reform without accounting for long-term stability.

Efficient Causes – How Post-Modernism Spreads

The ideology spreads not through conscious conspiracy but through **structural incentives**:

1. **Government Policies** – Welfare states, affirmative action, and bureaucratic expansion create dependencies on progressive ideology.
2. **Cultural Institutions** – Media, academia, and NGOs reinforce post-modernist dogma while demonizing dissent.
3. **Social Engineering** – Progressive norms dominate public discourse by labeling **alternative views as immoral or irrational.**

Final Causes – The Suppression of Dissent in the Name of Equality

Post-modernism claims to seek equality and justice, but its **true function is to eliminate differences, suppress opposition, and consolidate power.** Instead of uplifting people, it reduces society to the lowest common denominator by enforcing sameness.

- **Not a Utopia, but a Controlled Collapse** – The goal of post-modernism is not progress but dismantling functional structures in favor of ideological purity.
- **The Result: Social and Economic Decay** – By rejecting hierarchy, competence, and merit, post-modernism ensures its own destruction.

Part II: Post-Modernism, Wealth, and Entropy *(December 18, 2013)*

The Material Foundations of Civilization

Modern civilization is built on the accumulation of past knowledge, infrastructure, and labor - not spontaneous human progress. Wealth and stability are the result of past sacrifices, yet post-modernists take them for granted.

- **Specialization and Urbanization** – Economic growth has led to longer supply chains, greater interdependence, and detachment from production.
- **Intellectual Elites and the Loss of Practical Knowledge** – The ruling class, concentrated in cities, no longer understands basic survival needs, labor, or maintenance of civilization.

Entropy and the Illusion of Stability

Post-modernism flourishes because modern societies mistake artificial stability for a natural state of affairs.

Example: The Rural vs. Urban Divide

- A **rural homeowner** understands entropy: lawns must be mowed, fences must be repaired, and crops must be tended.
- A **city activist**, detached from physical maintenance, assumes order exists without labor, leading to policies that ignore consequences.

The Consequence: Utopian Policies That Undermine Reality

Progressive ideologues, detached from material reality, **promote policies that weaken the very systems that sustain them**:

- **Opposition to Fossil Fuels and GMOs** – A

failure to recognize the industrial systems that feed billions.

- **Hostility to Law Enforcement** – Ignoring that security requires control, not mere goodwill.
- **Redistribution Without Productivity** – Assuming wealth is infinite, rather than generated through work and innovation.

Part III: Post-Modernism's Final Causes and Pyrrhic Victory *(December 31, 2013)*

Does Post-Modernism Have a Purpose?

The author presents two possibilities:

- **Post-modernism is purely opportunistic**, promoting contradictory policies that serve power-holders.
- **It does have an ultimate goal** - a utopia where all social hierarchies are erased. However, this goal is self-defeating because redistribution itself creates new hierarchies and instability.

Post-Modernism's Self-Destructive Policies

By dismantling the institutions that sustain civilization, **post-modernism ensures its own downfall.**

- **Family Breakdown** – Undermining traditional family structures increases dependency on the state.

- **The Education Bubble** – Turning universities into ideological indoctrination centers inflates costs while devaluing real skills.
- **Declining Birth Rates** – Progressive societies encourage careerism over reproduction, leading to **demographic collapse.**
- **Mass Immigration as a Replacement Strategy** – Western societies, instead of addressing internal stagnation, **import populations with different cultural values that further destabilize them.**

The Pyrrhic Victory: Post-Modernism's Cannibalization of Itself

Post-modernism is winning battles but **losing the war.** It dominates cultural discourse, but by undermining **stability, order, and productivity**, it **dooms itself to irrelevance and collapse.**

- **Like a snake eating its own tail** – It destroys the very foundations that sustain it.
- **Like a crew burning its own ship** – It consumes resources without replenishing them, ensuring destruction.

Conclusion: The Fate of Post-Modernism

Post-modernism **thrives in excess** but **cannot survive scarcity.**

When **reality reasserts itself** (economic collapse, demographic crises, or civilizational breakdown), post-modernism **will be abandoned as a failed experiment.**

Key Takeaways from iParallax's Argument

- Post-modernism is an ideology born from excess. It can only exist in wealthy, stable societies where people forget that civilization must be maintained.
- It spreads by detaching elites from reality. Intellectuals, shielded from scarcity, **promote utopian policies that ignore trade-offs.**
- **It undermines the very conditions that allow it to exist.** By dismantling family structures, productive labor, and hierarchical order, post-modernism **guarantees its own collapse.**
- **It is inherently self-destructive.** Instead of building a new society, post-modernism **destroys functional systems without replacing them, ensuring its own failure.**
- It will not survive a return to material reality. Economic and demographic crises will expose its fundamental contradictions, leading to its decline.

Connect the Dots

Consider These Questions

- How does material prosperity allow bad ideas to spread?
- What happens when societies prioritize ideology over stability?
- Are today's progressive policies sustainable, or do they weaken the structures that make them possible?

- What historical examples show civilizations collapsing due to detachment from material reality?
- If post-modernism is doomed to collapse, what comes next?

Four Cases for Analysis:

- The Fall of the Weimar Republic and the Rise of the Nazi Regime (1919–1933)
- The 2008 Financial Crisis and the Education Bubble
- The Collapse of Venezuela's Economy (2010s)
- The European Migrant "Crisis" (2015–Present)

Short Works in the Neoreactionary Canon

"An Introduction to Group Dynamics" (2013) – nydwracu

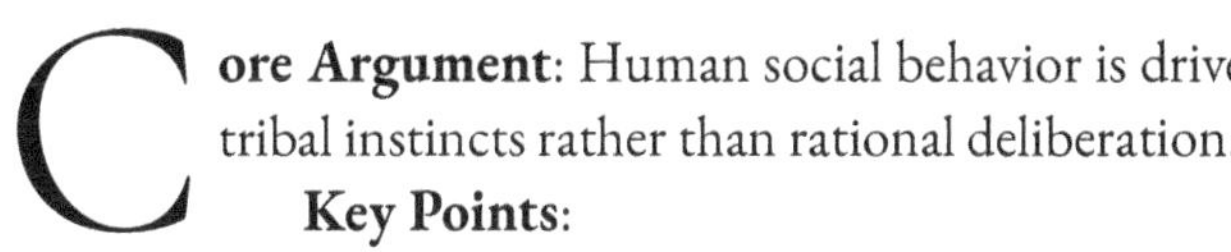

Core Argument: Human social behavior is driven by tribal instincts rather than rational deliberation.

Key Points:

- **Thedes vs. Elthedes**: Replaces in-group/out-group with "thedes" and "elthedes," emphasizing that people instinctively protect their own tribe.
- **Identity Over Logic**: Political allegiance is seen as a marker of social identity rather than a conclusion from rational discourse.
- **Language as Tribal Signal**: Speech norms solidify who's "in" or "out," undermining Enlightenment ideals of reasoned debate.
- **Critique of Rational Debate**: Argues that open discussion often fails because humans seek social belonging before truth.

Significance: Provides a theoretical basis for why modern democratic debate devolves into tribal identity politics instead of leading to rational consensus.

Flaws & Counterarguments:

Overstates Tribalness: Critics note that genuine ideological evolution does occur, as people can change their minds when presented with evidence.

Ignores Internal Divisions: Even within a single "thede," factions arise, suggesting more nuance than pure tribal affiliation.

"Material Conditions, Mass Psychology" (2013) – Amos & Gromar

Core Argument: Economic conditions shape ideological beliefs far more than reason or moral principles.

Key Points:

- **Complacency from Wealth**: In prosperous societies, people rarely question the political system.
- **Hardship as a Catalyst**: Economic crises can spur radical shifts as comfort erodes.
- **Academia as Status System**: Professors and scholars champion progressive ideas to gain prestige, not because they're always true.
- **Stability Enables Progressivism**: Progressive dominance is easier to maintain when basic needs are met.

Significance: Explains how economic comfort props up

progressive ideologies, implying that once comfort ends, progressive faith might crumble.

Flaws & Counterarguments:

Determinism: Not all economic downturns lead to reactionary politics; the 2008 recession saw left-wing populism instead.

Ignoring Blame Variance: People may blame corporations or capitalism rather than progressivism during crises, challenging the essay's assumption that progressivism fails first.

"How Democracy Fails: Brecht's Solution" (2013) – Wesley Morganston

Core Argument: Democracy is inherently unstable as politicians use demographic manipulation - like liberal immigration policies - to secure loyal voter bases.

Key Points:

- **Brecht's Poem**: Cites satirical notion of "dissolving the people and electing another."
- **Importing Voters**: Claims progressives encourage immigration to create a more compliant electorate.
- **Demographic Arms Race**: Democracy degenerates into competing attempts to reshape the population.
- **No Genuine Debate**: Outcomes hinge on who votes, not on which ideas win.

Significance: Reinforces the NRx argument that democracy inevitably collapses under attempts by elites to replace hostile constituents.

. . .

Flaws & Counterarguments:

Ignores Economic Motives: Immigration also serves business interests seeking cheap labor.

Monolithic Voting Blocs: Not all newcomers automatically vote left-wing, as real voter behavior can shift.

"The Part is Subordinate to the Whole: Female Outliers" (2013) – Amos & Gromar

Core Argument: Traditional patriarchal norms should remain despite the existence of exceptional women.

Key Points:

- **Gender Roles vs. Exceptions**: Admits some women outperform men but dismisses them as statistical anomalies.
- **Masculine Virtues**: Portrays attributes like honor or abstract thinking as innately male.
- **Collectivism Over Individualism**: Society's stability is deemed more vital than personal freedom for women.
- **Anti-Egalitarian**: Prefers patriarchal order, rejecting the concept of gender equality.

Significance: Offers a stark endorsement of patriarchy, prioritizing hierarchical gender roles over recognizing individual female talent.

Flaws & Counterarguments:

Oversimplifies Biology: Real-world data shows significant overlap between male and female capabilities.

Ignores Variation: Treats women as a monolith; does not address contexts where female leadership thrives.

"Language is a Badge of Tribal Membership" (2013) – Spandrell

Core Argument: Language primarily serves as a marker of group identity, and progressive language reforms are political tools.

Key Points:

- **Dialect = Identity**: People speak in ways that reinforce belonging, not necessarily for clarity.
- **Progressive Word-Policing**: Certain redefinitions (e.g., "racism = prejudice + power") act as ideological gatekeeping.
- **Elite English vs. Local Dialects**: Predicts a future global elite using one language while local tongues become resistance markers.
- **Political Tool**: Argues language can be weaponized to unify or marginalize groups.

Significance: Connects language politics to broader reactionary critiques of universalist progressivism, showing how words shape social power.

Flaws & Counterarguments:

Language Evolves Naturally Too: Not all changes are conspiratorial; many shifts arise from usage patterns.

Ignores Conservative Framing: Right-wing coinages (e.g., "death tax") also manipulate language.

"Three Reasons Diversity Isn't Working" (2013) – Wesley Morganston

Core Argument: Ethnic diversity undermines social trust and institutional performance.

Key Points:

- **Putnam's Findings**: Cites research on lower trust in diverse neighborhoods.
- **Institutional Priorities**: Diversity mandates can sideline competence or efficiency.
- **Forced Integration Backfires**: Mandated multiculturalism often fuels tension.
- **Homogeneity as Natural**: Suggests separating ethnic groups as a realistic solution.

Significance: Academic-style argument for restricting immigration and opposing affirmative diversity efforts, popular among ethno-nationalists.

Flaws & Counterarguments:

Selective Use of Putnam: He later noted that shared civic identity can mitigate distrust.

Successful Multiethnic Cases: Examples like Singapore or Switzerland challenge claims of inevitable fragmentation.

"Making Neoreaction Simple" (2013) – Amos & Gromar

Core Argument: Libertarians, who already accept inequality and decentralized structures, are the most likely to convert to neoreaction.

Key Points:

- **Libertarian Blind Spots**: Argues property-rights absolutism ignores real social failures.
- **Human Biodiversity**: Urges libertarians to incorporate racial and gender differences.
- **State Power**: Suggests a strong state or monarchy is still needed for order.
- **Conversion Strategy**: Sees libertarians as halfway to NRx, needing only a push.

Significance: Offers a rhetorical blueprint for recruiting from libertarian circles, bridging classical liberal economics and reactionary hierarchy.

Flaws & Counterarguments:

Tension with Libertarian Ethics: Minimizing personal liberty (through monarchy or patriarchy) conflicts with core libertarian principles.

Diverse Libertarian Thought: Many libertarians reject racial determinism, so the conversion pitch may be over-optimistic.

"The Cathedral and the Bizarre" (2013) – Wesley Morganston

Core Argument: Media and cultural narratives don't arise naturally but are carefully engineered by progressive institutions ("The Cathedral").

Key Points:

- **Trayvon Martin Example**: Frames the case as orchestrated media hype.
- **Decentralized Yet Unified**: Even Fox News implicitly follows progressive story framing.

- **Manufactured Consent**: Elite institutions shape "common sense," crowding out opposing views.
- **Conservative Capitulation**: Right-leaning media offers only token resistance.

Significance: Underlines neoreaction's core suspicion that a quasi-coordinated progressive establishment steers public discourse.

Flaws & Counterarguments:

Overgeneralization: Media outlets do clash; not all narratives align seamlessly.

Complex Motives: Cases like Trayvon Martin can reflect genuine public concern, not just top-down orchestration.

"A Decent Life for Decent People" (2013) – Handle's Haus

Core Argument: Public education is primarily about social control - containing disruptive youth - rather than genuine learning.

Key Points:

- **Containment Function**: Schools keep "bad kids" out of sight, preserving public order.
- **Reform Futility**: Fails because the real aim isn't academics but crowd control.
- **Progressive Taboo**: Race and behavioral differences can't be openly discussed.
- **Coded School Choice**: Parents pick "good schools" as a euphemism for safer, more homogenous demographics.

Significance: Reframes the education debate in purely social management terms, aligning with reactionary critiques of hidden policy motives.

Flaws & Counterarguments:

One-Dimensional: Overlooks success stories where public schools do improve outcomes.

Ignores Socioeconomic Factors: Crime and disruption often link to broader poverty or inequality issues, not just "bad kids."

"The Biological Vote" (2012) – The Social Pathologist

Core Argument: Political beliefs stem mostly from genetic or temperamental predispositions, making rational debate marginal.

Key Points:

- **Inherited Disposition**: Conservatives vs. liberals differ in openness and novelty response.
- **Tribal Democracy**: Voting aligns with innate personality traits, not reasoned policy analysis.
- **Progressive Overrunning**: Liberals adapt culture faster, pushing conservatives to adopt once-radical ideas.
- **Solutions**: Either a religious/ideological renaissance or a total democratic collapse.

Significance: Grounds reactionary skepticism in biological determinism, suggesting democracy cannot be "fixed" because it's shaped by inherent psychological traits.

. . .

Flaws & Counterarguments:

Overreliance on Genetics: Ignores social, cultural, and educational influences on political views.

Evidence Gaps: Genetic predisposition research is contested, and environment often overrides predispositions.

"THE MONKEY TRAP" (2013) – NICK LAND

Core Argument: Civilization halts the evolutionary pressures needed to develop higher intelligence, causing eventual cognitive decline.

Key Points:

- **Selection Pressure**: Intelligence evolves under brutal conditions where failure means death.
- **Dysgenic Stagnation**: Welfare and empathy reduce these pressures, stalling further cognitive gains.
- **Apex and Decay**: Social progress ironically fosters civilizational decay by removing harsh competition.
- **Cetacean Speculation**: Imagines a hypothetical future where dolphins might have evolved tool use and surpassed humanity.

Significance: Presents a fatalistic view of modern society as doomed to degrade intelligence, reinforcing the reactionary sense of inevitable decline.

Flaws & Counterarguments:

Flynn Effect: Real-world IQ trends complicate claims of universal dysgenic decline.

Tech-Driven Merit: Others argue advanced economies

reward intelligence in new ways, continuing selective pressures.

"Screwed Since 1913" (2013) – Wesley Morganston

Core Argument: WWI triggered a rift between American elites and common citizens, seeding modern progressive politics.

Key Points:

- **Republic to Empire**: Frames WWI as shifting the US from a smaller republic to a global empire.
- **Elitist Contempt**: Intellectuals turned away from uplifting the masses.
- **1965 Immigration Act**: Painted as demographic manipulation to restructure America.
- **Anti-Majoritarian**: Both left progressives and corporate right allegedly undermine native interests.

Significance: Provides a historical narrative for how elites supposedly built the progressive establishment post-WWI.

Flaws & Counterarguments:

Oversimplified History: WWI alone doesn't explain the vast changes wrought by industrialization, the Great Depression, or WWII.

Lack of Evidence: The 1965 Act was multifaceted; the claim of deliberate new-elector creation is debated.

"Creeping Horror" (2014) – Free Northerner

Core Argument: Systematic distortions in mainstream media erode public knowledge, suggesting deeper institutional dysfunction.

Key Points:

- **Compare Expertise**: Encourages readers to scrutinize news coverage of their own specialty.
- **Widespread Ignorance**: Concludes journalists, and thus the public, are misinformed across many domains.
- **Institutional Rot**: Suggests a permanent gap between reality and mainstream narrative.
- **Skepticism**: Encourages doubting any official consensus.

Significance: Bolsters the NRx stance that "The Cathedral" operates through incompetent or biased media, justifying alternative information channels.

Flaws & Counterarguments:

Overgeneralizes: Not all media coverage is equally poor; some outlets incorporate expert commentary.

Confirmation Bias: Even reactionary sources can harbor distortions, so universal skepticism cuts both ways.

"Myth, Rhetoric, and the Dark Enlightenment" (2013) – Habitable Worlds

Core Argument: Politics runs on emotionally powerful myths; purely rational arguments rarely mobilize mass support.

Key Points:

- **Progressive Moral Universe**: The left's success attributed to framing issues as moral battles.
- **Right's Failure**: Reactionaries rely on dry facts, missing emotional resonance.
- **Need for Myth**: Encourages NRx to craft compelling narratives of its own.
- **Plato's Phaedrus Reference**: Dialectic alone is insufficient; persuasion must accompany truth.

Significance: Urges reactionaries to adopt myth-making strategies akin to progressive moral storytelling, bridging rhetorical gaps.

Flaws & Counterarguments:

Contradiction with Elitism: If the masses are unworthy, why bother persuading them?

Material vs. Myth: Overstates rhetorical skill as key; real factors like economic interest and institutions also shape success.

"INACCESSIBLE IS UNGOVERNABLE" (2013) – HANDLE'S HAUS

Core Argument: Modern states' excessive complexity makes them ungovernable, as no one fully understands the regulatory maze.

Key Points:

- **Regulatory Avalanche**: Layers of rules accumulate faster than any official can track.
- **Opacity and Arbitrary Power**: Complexity fosters selective enforcement.
- **Simplicity or Collapse**: Argues for radical downsizing of governance.
- **Aligns with Anti-Democratic**: Another reason democracy fails: it spawns unwieldy bureaucracies.

Significance: Targets the structural inefficiency of democratic governments, reinforcing the case for simpler, centralized authority.

Flaws & Counterarguments:

Autocracies Also Complex: Historical monarchies or dictatorships also created labyrinthine bureaucracies.

Potential Tech Solutions: Digital governance or AI could help manage complexity rather than requiring total rollback.

"CHINESE EUGENICS AND WHY LOSERS DON'T WIN" (2013) – WESLEY MORGANSTON

Core Argument: China's readiness to pursue genetic research for intelligence enhancement gives it an edge over a morally constrained West.

Key Points:

- **IQ as Key Resource**: Views intelligence as the primary driver of societal success.
- **Western Taboos**: Progressive ethics block open research on eugenics.
- **Competitive Edge**: China's "pragmatic" approach will yield superior elites.
- **Ethical Dismissal**: Frames Western caution as irrational fear or moral posturing.

Significance: Places eugenics at the center of a future global power struggle, highlighting NRx acceptance of selective breeding.

Flaws & Counterarguments:

Overlooks Complexity: Intelligence research is nuanced; environment and education matter too.

Ethical Oversight: Dismisses legitimate worries about inequality, genetic diversity, and unintended consequences.

"Monarchy" (2013) – Spandrell

Core Argument: Monarchy's hereditary succession fosters continuity, stability, and social cohesion, unlike democracy's factional chaos.

Key Points:

- **Evolution from Warlords**: Monarchies often arise from successful military figures.

- **Succession Certainty**: Dynastic lines remove repeated leadership contests.
- **Japan as Example**: The imperial family's symbolic power survived massive political change.
- **Schelling Point**: People naturally rally around a king in uncertain times.

Significance: Proposes monarchy as an explicitly stable alternative to democratic churn, illustrating one possible reactionary governance model.

Flaws & Counterarguments:

Historical Tyranny: Many monarchies were corrupt or incompetent, undermining claims of inherent stability.

Modern Irrelevance: Adapting monarchy to large, complex 21st-century societies is vague.

"Burnout" (2013) – nydwracu

Core Argument: Liberal democracy extinguishes the evolutionary fire that drives excellence, fostering cultural stagnation.

Key Points:

- **Welfare Indulgence**: People settle into mediocrity if guaranteed resources.
- **Merit Eroded**: Competitive drive dissolves under egalitarian aims.
- **Cultural Decay**: Society "burns out" rather than evolves.
- **Return to Hierarchy**: Implies we need a system that rewards strong performers.

Significance: Extends the recurring NRx theme that

modern civilization, by reducing hardship, undermines the impetus for growth.

Flaws & Counterarguments:

Simplistic: Blames "comfort" for all decline, ignoring that stable societies can still innovate.

Ignores Progressive Achievements: Many major breakthroughs occurred under liberal democracies with robust welfare systems.

"CIPHER IDEOLOGY" (2013) – BRYCE LALIBERTE

Core Argument: Neoreaction is a transformative "meta-ideology" that modernist paradigms cannot fully grasp or refute.

Key Points:

- **Lovecraftian Horror**: Once you realize NRx's premises, you cannot "unsee" them.
- **Esoteric Stance**: Advocates deliberately resisting mass acceptance.
- **Outside Modernist Critique**: Mainstream cannot effectively critique what it cannot conceptualize.
- **Intellectual Virus**: NRx frames itself as an unassailable mindset.

Significance: Serves as a self-justification for NRx's contrarian stance, reinforcing an elitist or "occultic" identity.

Flaws & Counterarguments:

Immunity Claim: Claiming no mainstream critique can touch NRx can appear as dogmatic self-sealing.

Elitist Bubble: Encouraging esotericism may limit practical influence.

"HORRORISM" (2013) – NICK LAND

Core Argument: Neoreaction should spread existential dread ("horrorism") rather than strive for traditional political activism.

Key Points:

- **Contrast with Terrorism**: Instead of violence, sow deep fatalism about progressive solutions.
- **Despair as Weapon**: Tells opponents, "Nothing you do will work," undermining morale.
- **Accelerationist Flavor**: Passive approach lets the system collapse.
- **Anti-Mass Action**: Rejects typical movement-building in favor of psychological subversion.

Significance: Pioneers a nihilistic strategic stance within NRx, advocating psychological warfare over direct engagement.

Flaws & Counterarguments:

Neglects Constructive Goals: Sowing despair doesn't outline a stable future system.

Might Backfire: Encouraging cynicism could alienate potential allies or bolster other extremist movements.

"The Cult of Neoreaction" (2013) – Samo Burja

Core Argument: NRx risks devolving into a subcultural "cult" rather than evolving into a serious intellectual or political force.

Key Points:

- **Debate Between Leaders**: Mentions tensions over intellectual rigor vs. popularization.
- **Warnings Against Insularity**: Becoming a fandom hinders real-world impact.
- **Need Institutions**: Calls for sustained scholarly structures and debate.
- **Fear of Nerd Culture**: Online echo chambers hamper deeper analysis.

Significance: Provides an internal critique urging NRx to avoid turning into a niche internet clique, aiming instead for institutional heft.

Flaws & Counterarguments:

Movement Dilemma: Balancing public reach with intellectual purity is a common challenge for any ideology.

Lack of Practical Steps: Critique doesn't specify how to build those serious institutions.

"Neoreaction, Liberalism, Conservatism: Reject the Isms" (2013) – Amos & Gromar

Core Argument: Neoreaction is distinct from (and superior to) both liberalism and conservatism because it recognizes power, class systems, and patriarchy as indispensable.

Key Points:

- **Critique of Conservatism**: Mainstream right is intellectually shallow, failing to address core issues.
- **Progressivism's Errors**: Believes liberals misdiagnose social problems.
- **Affirmation of Patriarchy**: Patriarchal and hierarchical norms are vital.
- **Rejecting Harm Principle**: Emphasizes collective good over individuals' negative liberties.

Significance: Establishes NRx as a fundamental break from older right-wing or liberal traditions, highlighting patriarchy and class as non-negotiable.

Flaws & Counterarguments:

Dismissive of Mainstream: Overlooks complex intellectual strands within conservatism and liberalism.

Ethical Gaps: Minimizes potential abuses under patriarchy or rigid hierarchy.

"UR-MALTHUSIANISM" (2013) – BRYCE LALIBERTE

Core Argument: Technological progress and welfare undermine natural Malthusian selection, yielding dysgenic outcomes.

Key Points:

- **Disrupted Selection**: Society extends lifespans artificially, allowing less fit individuals to proliferate.

- **Downward Spiral**: Over time, average capability declines.
- **Controlled Tech**: Suggests limiting or channeling technology to preserve selective pressures.
- **Hints of Eugenics**: Implies a preference for deliberate breeding strategies.

Significance: Another example of NRx integrating classical Malthusian logic with modern welfare critiques, reinforcing eugenic undertones.

Flaws & Counterarguments:

Counter-Evidence: Rising global IQ in many regions defies pure Malthusian claims.

Moral Dimension: Dismisses ethical concerns around enforced "selection."

"Taking on the Cathedral" (2013) – The Social Pathologist

Core Argument: Advocates a decentralized "guerrilla" cultural strategy to avoid direct confrontation with mainstream progressive (Cathedral) institutions.

Key Points:

- **Michael Collins Analogy**: Stresses infiltration and sabotage over open political battles.
- **Media Trap**: Engaging mainstream outlets ensures distortion.
- **Online & Local Tactics**: Use internet-based networks to quietly build alternative narratives.
- **Avoiding High Profile**: Big organizations become easy Cathedral targets.

Significance: Provides a practical “underground” strategy for NRx activism, paralleling historical guerrilla warfare.

Flaws & Counterarguments:

Limited Reach: Going underground might also limit mainstream influence.

Echo Chamber Risk: Decentralized sabotage can devolve into insular internet cliques rather than broad transformation.

"Transhumanism and Palingenesis" (2013) – Michael Anissimov

Core Argument: Radical techno-breakthroughs could spark a civilizational rebirth (palingenesis) aligned with reactionary ideals.

Key Points:

- **Two Transhumanist Approaches**: Gradual vs. sudden “singularity.”
- **Tech & Governance**: Each system - liberal, authoritarian, or reactionary - would harness breakthroughs differently.
- **NRx Opportunity**: An advanced monarchy or corporate state might accelerate post-human evolution.
- **Ethical Oversight**: Minimally addressed, focusing on strategic advantage.

Significance: Bridges futuristic transhumanism with reactionary politics, implying an elite, high-tech post-democratic order.

. . .

Flaws & Counterarguments:

Idealized: Tech breakthroughs may not align with hierarchical visions; progressive innovators also exist.

Ethical Blind Spots: Overlooks inequality and potential for "techno-tyranny."

"A Typology of Magic" (2013) – nydwracu

Core Argument: Ideological conflict can be understood in terms of "magic," with rhetorical operations shaping what's thinkable.

Key Points:

- **Black Magic**: Exposing taboo truths (e.g., The Cathedral) that mainstream tries to hide.
- **White Magic**: Building new frameworks of meaning - terms, narratives - that shape public thought.
- **Four Operations**: Invention, Reinforcement, Reversal, Erasure detail how language warfare unfolds.
- **Memetic Power**: Encourages reactionaries to craft or reclaim key terms.

Significance: Provides an analytic lens for rhetorical manipulation, relevant to NRx strategies of infiltration and conceptual sabotage.

Flaws & Counterarguments:

Highly Abstract: "Magic" is metaphorical; critics might say it oversimplifies complex sociopolitical processes.

Two-Way Street: Progressives and reactionaries alike can employ such tactics, so it's not uniquely NRx.

"Discrimination" (2013) – Nick Land

Core Argument: Discrimination is a natural, even virtuous, exercise in discerning threats or quality, and progressives invert this moral order.

Key Points:

- **Caplan Critique**: Rejects the idea that misanthropy is worse than tribal prejudice.
- **Moral Inversion**: Anti-discrimination norms punish prudent judgment.
- **Hierarchy Affirmation**: Equates discrimination with intelligent selection.
- **Survival Utility**: Argues communities that fail to discriminate weaken themselves.

Significance: Defends discrimination as a constructive social force, aligning with the NRx endorsement of hierarchy.

Flaws & Counterarguments:

Risk of Abuse: Historically, "discrimination" fostered severe oppression (racism, sexism, xenophobia).

Selective Logic: Overlooking contexts where open-mindedness or diversity spurred innovation and resilience.

"Orwell and Newspeak" (2013) – The Social Pathologist

Core Argument: Newspeak arises organically in democracies as leaders cater to a cognitively limited "prole-mind," rather than via totalitarian decree.

Key Points:

- **Bottom-Up Simplification**: The masses prefer neat slogans, fueling simplistic language.
- **Orwell's Mistake**: Contradicts the notion of imposed Newspeak from above.
- **Prole Appeal**: Politicians feed easy narratives to cognitively lazy voters.
- **Supports Anti-Democracy**: Another reason democracy fails - people want trivial language.

Significance: Reiterates the theme that democratic debate degenerates due to mass intellectual limitations rather than direct censorship.

Flaws & Counterarguments:

Ignores Top-Down Influence: Governments and corporations can still impose terms or rhetorical frames.

Civic Education: Some argue better public education counters reductive language norms.

"WITTGENSTEIN, IDEOLOGY, AND SIGNALING" (2014) – BRYCE LALIBERTE

Core Argument: All political stances occupy ideologically bound "language games"; no view is purely neutral.

Key Points:

- **Living Ideology**: Worldviews adapt reflexively to internal contradictions.
- **Wittgenstein's Legacy**: Meaning depends on context; no universal rational vantage.
- **Signaling**: People adopt beliefs to show group loyalty, not pure logic.

- **NRx Embrace**: Urges acceptance of NRx as explicitly ideological.

Significance: Lays a philosophical foundation for NRx's self-awareness about being an ideology outside the mainstream.

Flaws & Counterarguments:

Undermining Universal Claims: If all stances are language games, NRx's own claims are likewise "non-neutral."

Practical Solutions?: Embracing ideology doesn't explain how to govern effectively.

"Clausewitz, Lenin, Robin Dunbar" (2013) – Spandrell

Core Argument: Power is decided by personal alliances and tribal jockeying, not high-minded principles or popular will.

Key Points:

- **Clausewitz & Lenin**: War and revolution revolve around forging strong, loyal cadres.
- **Dunbar's Number**: Elites maintain cohesive networks of ~150 close contacts.
- **Tribal Reality**: Public "issues" cloak interpersonal alliances in moral language.
- **Democracy as Illusion**: True power rests with behind-the-scenes social alliances.

Significance: Underscores an NRx staple: modern democracy is a façade for elite tribal negotiations, not a real marketplace of ideas.

. . .

Flaws & Counterarguments:

Oversimplification: Does not fully account for institutional checks, public mobilization, or ideology's genuine influence.

Elite Rivalries: Even small elites can fracture, undermining the notion of stable alliances.

"The Dove Sketches Beauty Scam" (2013) – The Last Psychiatrist

Core Argument: Corporate marketing hijacks progressive ideals like body positivity to manipulate consumers for profit.

Key Points:

- **Confidence Trick**: The "Real Beauty" campaign is structured like a short con, selling "validation."
- **Self-Esteem Debt**: People accumulate unearned psychological reassurance from ads.
- **Authority Transfer**: Dove becomes the new "standard-setter" of beauty.
- **Reinforcing Norms**: Consumers think they resist beauty culture but actually bolster it by trusting Dove.

Significance: Demonstrates how capitalism can co-opt progressive rhetoric, aligning with NRx suspicion that mainstream institutions are ideologically hollow.

Flaws & Counterarguments:

Consumers Not Passive: Many do question or subvert ad messaging.

Commercial Complexity: Marketing can be interpretive;

some see value in body-positive campaigns despite corporate motives.

"Real Men Want To Drink Guinness..." (2013) – The Last Psychiatrist

Core Argument: Modern advertising exploits insecure men's desire for a performative form of masculinity.

Key Points:

- **Guinness Wheelchair Ad**: Depicts camaraderie to reassure men of "good-guy" masculinity.
- **Male Insecurity**: Beta males seek external confirmation rather than genuine self-confidence.
- **Cadillac Comparison**: Contrasts a more blatantly manipulative ad targeting female frustration with weak men.
- **Symbolic Virtue**: Men are trained to show masculinity symbolically rather than living it authentically.

Significance: Reveals a marketing tactic that NRx interprets as undermining genuine masculinity, fueling a cultural sense of male decline.

Flaws & Counterarguments:

Interpretive Subjectivity: Ads can be read differently; not all men see the Guinness ad as masculine reassurance.

Ignores Positive Interpretations: Some see the ad as championing inclusivity or genuine friendship.

"TO LIGHT A FIRE UNDER THE ASS OF THE NEOREACTION" (2013) – RAPTROS

Core Argument: The West is in terminal decline; NRx must shift from philosophical debate to real-world action.

Key Points:

- **Alarmist Tone**: Portrays civilizational collapse as imminent.
- **Two Options**: "Fight" by accelerating the fall or "Exit" to enclaves that preserve traditional knowledge.
- **Evola Influence**: Cites spiritual or metaphysical struggle as a higher calling.
- **Calls for Urgency**: Criticizes endless theory, demanding a practical reactionary movement.

Significance: Pushes NRx toward activism, bridging intangible critique with on-the-ground preparation for societal breakdown.

Flaws & Counterarguments:

Vague Implementation: Lacks specifics on how to mount large-scale fight or coordinate enclaves.

Crisis Not Guaranteed: Societies have faced challenges before without total meltdown.

"GAME, DARK ENLIGHTENMENT, AND REACTION" (2013) – JIM

Core Argument: Insights from the "manosphere" (pickup artist tactics) confirm that patriarchy is necessary, and democracy fails when women hold political power.

Key Points:

- **Female Hypergamy**: Suggests women inherently seek dominant men, needing male authority.
- **Emotional Voting**: Asserts that women vote for redistribution and social welfare, destabilizing economies.
- **Self-Destructive Feminine**: Unchecked female autonomy allegedly leads to social chaos.
- **Gateway to Reaction**: Studying "Game" fosters a realization that patriarchy is "correct."

Significance: Merges the PUA/manosphere subculture with NRx theory, reinforcing misogynistic or patriarchal arguments against female political participation.

Flaws & Counterarguments:

Misogynistic Generalizations: Overlooks data on women's diverse voting patterns and leadership successes.

Reductionist: Reduces complex social issues to sexual competition or "hypergamy."

KEY THEMES & CONCLUDING REMARKS

Throughout these shorter works, **five overarching themes** emerge:

1. **Anti-Democratic Critique**: Democracy is portrayed as doomed to corruption, manipulated by elites or short-sighted masses.
2. **Pro-Hierarchy**: Advocates monarchy, patriarchy, or corporate rule as more "natural" and stable than equality-based systems.

3. **Biological Determinism**: Emphasis on racial, sexual, or genetic differences as major drivers of societal outcomes.
4. **Hostility to Progressive Institutions**: Argues "The Cathedral" (media, academia, bureaucracy) enforces an egalitarian ideology that suppresses dissent.
5. **Strategic Outlook**: From rhetorical "magic" to stealth "guerrilla" infiltration, authors propose varied tactics for reactionary victory post-collapse.

Critical Observations:

Lack of Practical Implementation: Many authors critique democracy but provide limited specifics on how monarchy or patriarchy would function in a modern, pluralistic society.

Selective Data Use: IQ studies, Putnam's research, or evolutionary psychology are often cited in ways critics say are cherry-picked.

Contradictory Stances: Some texts call for esoteric elitism, others for broad activism.

Focus on Collapse: Commonly predict or even welcome societal breakdown as the impetus for reactionary "restoration."

These short works thus deepen the broader Neoreactionary Canon, blending philosophy, social critique, and strategic planning. While they raise thoughtful points on institutional flaws and mass psychology, they also exhibit potential weaknesses in evidence, moral justification, and real-world feasibility.

Conclusion

The Endgame of Neoreactionary Thought

Curtis Yarvin's *Neoreactionary Canon* is not a rigorous political treatise. It is a persuasive effort - one designed to **convince, reframe, and radicalize** rather than to engage in genuine debate. His work is most effective not because it presents historically or politically sound ideas, but because it reshapes old reactionary principles into something palatable for modern audiences - particularly in tech and elite business circles, where skepticism toward democracy already exists in various forms.

The Core Takeaways

Across this book, we have broken down **Yarvin's central arguments**, examined their **historical flaws**, and deconstructed **his rhetorical techniques**. The major themes of his work can be distilled into the following key takeaways:

. . .

Democracy Is an Illusion, and Rule by Elites Is Inevitable.

Yarvin argues that democracy is merely a façade, controlled by entrenched bureaucratic elites (*The Cathedral*). His solution? Hand power over to an explicit, permanent ruling class, whether a corporate CEO, a king, or an elite aristocracy.

Government Should Be Run Like a Corporation.

This is a rebranding of monarchy in tech-world language. By replacing the language of "king" with "sovereign CEO" and "aristocracy" with "stakeholders," Yarvin attempts to make autocracy sound like an efficiency upgrade.

Voting Rights Should Be Restricted - or Abolished Entirely.

While he dances around this idea, the logical conclusion of his work is that democracy cannot be saved. He presents various alternatives - restricting suffrage to property owners, "intelligent" voters, or dissolving elections entirely in favor of corporate governance.

Diversity and Universal Rights Are Flaws, Not Strengths.

Yarvin's work is laced with *human biodiversity* (HBD) arguments, where he suggests - often indirectly - that certain groups are naturally predisposed to rule while others are not. He portrays homogeneity as politically necessary while downplaying the successes of diverse democracies.

If You Can't Reform the System, Exit It.

A key part of Yarvin's solution is "exit" - abandoning democratic governance altogether. Whether through **seasteading**, **startup societies**, or **corporate states**, he encourages wealthy elites to withdraw from democratic systems rather than attempt to change them.

The Grand Contradiction: Who Governs the Governors?

One of the most glaring weaknesses in Yarvin's worldview is that **he never fully answers the fundamental question of power: What happens when his "sovereign CEO" fails, becomes corrupt, or acts against the interests of his subjects?**

- In democratic systems, power is checked by elections, legal institutions, and public accountability.
- In Yarvin's world, **power is absolute** - and he assumes, without much evidence, that this will somehow produce competent rulers.

History does not support this assumption. The strongest autocratic states (from the Habsburgs to modern Singapore) have thrived **not because of unchecked power, but because of strong bureaucratic and institutional frameworks** - which Yarvin largely dismisses as part of *The Cathedral.*

This is the **fatal contradiction** of neoreactionary thought:

- Yarvin argues that **bureaucratic elites already rule behind the scenes** - but rather than addressing corruption or improving accountability, he simply wants to make elite rule *explicit and permanent.*

- He claims to **oppose elite manipulation** while simultaneously arguing that the masses should have no say in governance at all.
- He presents himself as an **anti-utopian realist** while selling a vision of government that assumes rulers will always act in long-term good faith - a deeply utopian belief.

The reality is that **unchecked power breeds corruption, no matter who holds it**. There is no reason to believe that a tech CEO or a hereditary monarch will make decisions any better than an elected official - especially when those in power face no consequences for failure.

Yarvin's Real-World Influence: Why This Matters

Yarvin himself is not in power, but his ideas **are already influencing elites** in ways that shape **tech, politics, and finance**:

- **Peter Thiel**, the billionaire venture capitalist, has publicly echoed Yarvin's skepticism of democracy and belief in strong executives. Thiel's investments in political candidates who favor centralized power (such as J.D. Vance) suggest that these ideas are trickling into real governance.
- **Startup societies, charter cities, and exit strategies** are being explored by groups attempting to create autonomous corporate-run territories free from democratic oversight.
- **The tech-right movement**, including figures in Silicon Valley and crypto circles, is increasingly drawn to Yarvin's critiques of democracy, seeing them as justification for elite-led governance.

In short, *Yarvin's ideas are not just theoretical - they are aspirational blueprints for certain factions of the billionaire class*. While Yarvin himself remains a niche figure, the broader sentiment he represents - **the desire for a world ruled by "rational" elites rather than elected officials** - is gaining traction in business and political circles.

What Comes Next? The Future of Neoreactionary Thought

So where does this all lead? If Yarvin's ideas continue gaining influence among political and business elites, several possible outcomes emerge:

- **More attempts to create "exit" societies** - privatized city-states, charter cities, and autonomous corporate enclaves where democracy is removed entirely.
- **A stronger push toward elite-driven politics** - with billionaires funding candidates who favor "strongman" governance over participatory democracy.
- **Tech-led governance experiments** - where AI, automation, and algorithmic rule are used as a justification to remove human decision-making from politics.

However, history suggests that **anti-democratic movements inevitably face resistance**. People do not easily accept being ruled without consent, and every past attempt to consolidate power in a ruling elite - whether feudalism, aristocracy, or fascism - has eventually been met with revolt or collapse.

Final Thoughts: Understanding Without Mythologizing

Yarvin's work is seductive because it offers **a simplistic narrative**:

1. That democracy is an illusion.
2. That a competent ruler can "fix" government.
3. That rule by elites is inevitable.

But political reality is far messier. The problems of democracy - corruption, inefficiency, bureaucratic stagnation - are real. But the answer is not **autocracy wrapped in corporate jargon**.

The real takeaway from Yarvin's work is not that his ideas should be **implemented**, but that they should be **understood, scrutinized, and resisted where necessary**. His ability to shape elite discourse shows that reactionary politics do not need mass movements to succeed - they only need **enough billionaires, technocrats, and policymakers to find them useful**.

This book has aimed to provide a **clear, structured counterpoint** to Yarvin's ideas, separating what is insightful from what is deceptive. The final question to ask is this:

If democracy is flawed but better than dictatorship, **what should be done to fix it** - rather than abandon it?

Because in the end, that is the real choice at stake.

Glossary of Neoreactionary & Yarvinite Terms

This glossary provides definitions and explanations of Curtis Yarvin's (Mencius Moldbug) core concepts, as well as key terms from the broader Neoreactionary (NRx) movement and its offshoots. Many of these terms were coined or adapted by Yarvin and his intellectual allies to frame their arguments and critique democracy, liberalism, and modern governance.

A

Accelerationism

A philosophy, associated with Nick Land, that suggests modernity and capitalism should be pushed to their limits to accelerate collapse and transformation. In NRx, this often means embracing the collapse of liberal democracy so that an authoritarian, hierarchical alternative can emerge.

The Administrative State

A derogatory term for the modern bureaucratic government, which NRx thinkers argue wields real power rather than elected officials. Often used interchangeably with "The Managerial State."

Anarcho-Monarchism

A seemingly contradictory term sometimes used in NRx to describe the idea that a sovereign monarch should rule absolutely, but without micromanaging the daily lives of citizens. Essentially, it's an extreme form of **laissez-faire governance** under an absolute ruler.

B

Bailey and Motte Tactics

A rhetorical strategy often attributed to progressives but recognized and adopted by reactionaries. The "motte" is a defensible, reasonable claim, while the "bailey" is a more extreme position. When challenged, the advocate retreats to the motte but continues advancing the bailey when unchallenged. Neoreactionaries claim this tactic is used to push progressive ideals under the guise of moderate rhetoric.

Biological Realism

A euphemism used in NRx to argue that genetics shape political and social behavior, often in racial and gendered terms. This overlaps with the fringe **Human Biodiversity (HBD) movement**, which claims that innate biological differences justify hierarchies in governance, intelligence, and social structures.

Black Magic

A term used within neoreactionary thought, particularly by **nydwracu**, to describe the act of revealing hidden ideological structures and naming forbidden truths. In this framework, **black magic** works by exposing the concealed mechanisms of power - such as "The Cathedral" - forcing people to recognize realities they were conditioned to ignore.

It is contrasted with **white magic**, which reinforces the dominant ideology.

C

The Cathedral

Yarvin's term for the self-reinforcing ideological system of **universities, media, and bureaucracy**, which he claims dictates public opinion and suppresses dissenting thought. According to Yarvin, the Cathedral is an informal but powerful network that enforces progressive ideology through cultural and institutional control rather than direct coercion.

Clear Pill

Yarvin's term for his updated philosophy on power, described in *The Clear Pill* (2021). It builds on his earlier *red pill* ideas but reframes political struggle as not a battle between right and left but between **power and illusion**. He argues that democracy is performative, and real power operates behind the scenes.

Cognitive Misers

A psychological concept repurposed by neoreactionaries to argue that most people are incapable of rational, independent thought. Instead, they rely on prepackaged ideological narratives, making them easily manipulated by institutions like The Cathedral.

Corporate Sovereignty

A foundational idea in Yarvin's *Neocameralism*, where a state should be run like a **private corporation**, with a CEO (sovereign) governing as the sole decision-maker, much like a monarch. Governance should be treated as an economic enterprise rather than a democratic process.

D

The Dark Enlightenment

A term popularized by Nick Land to describe the **intellectual movement rejecting democracy, egalitarianism, and liberal modernity**. The name suggests an inverse of the Enlightenment, embracing hierarchy, authoritarian rule, and reactionary ideas.

Demotism

A pejorative NRx term for **any system of government that appeals to mass participation** (i.e., democracy, socialism, populism). Demotism is considered inherently unstable because it prioritizes public opinion over competent rule.

Distributed Despotism

A concept that argues modern liberal democracies operate like decentralized dictatorships, where bureaucratic elites and the media hold **real power** rather than elected officials. In this view, the U.S. President is a figurehead, while unelected elites enforce ideological conformity.

E

Exit vs. Voice

A concept borrowed from Albert O. Hirschman but reframed by Yarvin.

Voice refers to **participating in democracy** (e.g., voting, activism, reform). Yarvin argues this is useless because democratic institutions are designed to **absorb and neutralize dissent**.

Exit means **leaving the system entirely**, either through secession, private governance, or the creation of **alternative political structures** (e.g., seasteading, startup cities). Yarvin sees **exit** as the only viable path for change.

F

Formalism

Yarvin's belief that **political power should be made explicit and structured like property ownership**. Instead of pretending that elected officials represent the people, it is better to acknowledge that **rulers own the state**. This is the ideological basis for **Neocameralism**, where governance is corporate and transparent.

G

Gray Magic

A hybrid of **black** and **white magic**, gray magic involves subtly manipulating ideological narratives without completely breaking with the dominant order. This can include subverting progressive discourse from within or using ambiguity to advance reactionary ideas under the guise of neutrality.

H

Hestia Strategy

A specific form of passivism that encourages individuals to focus on building **small-scale, self-sustaining reactionary communities** rather than engaging with mainstream politics. The name "Hestia" (from the Greek goddess of the hearth) symbolizes retreating from public life to cultivate private, hierarchical orders.

Human Biodiversity (HBD)

A controversial term that promotes **genetic explanations for political and social differences**, often used in racial and gendered contexts. While not unique to NRx, it is frequently cited by Yarvin-adjacent thinkers to justify hierarchical governance.

Hyperstition

A concept borrowed from accelerationist philosophy, meaning a **belief that creates its own reality**. Yarvin argues that progressive dominance is maintained **not through force, but through the hyperstitious belief that democracy is legitimate**. By shifting how elites think about power, he hopes to create a new political order.

M

The Managerial State

A concept borrowed from James Burnham's *The Managerial Revolution* (1941), describing a government where real power is held by **bureaucrats, administrators, and corporate elites**, not by elected officials. Yarvin claims this system creates **unaccountable governance**, which democracy cannot fix.

Moldbuggian Rhetoric

A term used to describe Yarvin's **long-winded, deliberately digressive writing style**, designed to gradually guide readers toward radical conclusions. His rhetorical tactics include:

1 **Historical reframing** (e.g., portraying monarchy as more stable than democracy).

2 **Tech-friendly metaphors** (e.g., describing governance as a "software update").

3 **Elitist appeal** (framing reactionary ideas as *esoteric knowledge* for the intelligent few).

N

Neocameralism

Yarvin's proposed alternative to democracy. It envisions a **state run like a private corporation**, with a single **sovereign CEO** instead of an elected government. Citizens would be like customers or employees rather than voters, and governance would prioritize efficiency over public input.

NRx (Neoreaction)

A broad intellectual movement that includes Yarvin's ideas but also incorporates:

Techno-commercialists (favoring CEO-run governance).

Theonomists (Christian traditionalists advocating theocratic rule).

Ethno-nationalists (who focus on race as the basis for governance). The movement is deeply **anti-democratic, anti-egalitarian, and pro-hierarchy**.

O

Overton Window

The range of ideas considered acceptable in mainstream political discourse. NRx thinkers seek to **shift the Overton Window rightward**, making authoritarianism, monarchy, and elite rule more palatable.

P

Passivism

A strategy advocated by Curtis Yarvin, arguing that political change should not come from direct activism but rather from **withdrawing support from the system** until it collapses under its own contradictions. Unlike traditional activism, which seeks reform, passivism holds that the system is beyond saving and must be allowed to fail before a new order can emerge.

Patchwork

Yarvin's vision for a world without **large, centralized states**. Instead, he proposes a fragmented map of **small, independent corporate-governed city-states** that compete for residents like businesses compete for customers. The idea is inspired by the historical Holy Roman Empire and Singapore-style governance.

S

Sovereign Corporation

A term in Neocameralism describing a **government that operates like a private company**, with a CEO-style ruler and total centralization of power. Yarvin sees this as an alternative to both democracy and traditional monarchy.

T

Thede / Elthedes

A conceptual framework from **nydwracu** that replaces the traditional "in-group" and "out-group" terminology. A **thede** refers to a group united by shared cultural, ethnic, or ideological bonds, while an **elthedes** is an out-group with whom one's thede is in conflict. This framework is used to analyze political and cultural tribalism.

Toxoplasma of Rage

A term derived from Scott Alexander's *Slate Star Codex*, used in neoreactionary discourse to describe the way social media amplifies controversy and outrage, reinforcing ideological division. The phrase is based on the idea that some memes or ideas "infect" public discourse, ensuring maximum polarization.

Transcameralism

A lesser-known term that builds on **Neocameralism**, exploring how digital and decentralized technologies (e.g., blockchain governance, DAOs) might replace **traditional state structures**. Some Yarvin-adjacent thinkers see this as a futuristic path beyond monarchy.

. . .

W

W-Force

A term occasionally referenced in reactionary circles to describe the **underlying forces that drive history toward order, hierarchy, and reaction**. It is often invoked as a vague **metaphysical force** pulling society away from progressive decay and toward a "restored" traditional order.

Warg

A derogatory neoreactionary term for those who attempt to engage in progressive activism within reactionary spaces or who fail to grasp the deeply hierarchical and deterministic worldview of neoreaction. The term is adapted from fantasy literature (notably *Game of Thrones*), where "wargs" are beings who attempt to control others through possession.

White Magic

Thc counterpart to **black magic**, white magic refers to the linguistic and ideological operations that sustain the dominant progressive ideology. It includes the creation of new ideological terms (e.g., "white privilege"), the reinforcement of existing social norms, and the suppression of dissenting viewpoints through rhetorical framing.

Final Thoughts

This glossary provides the essential terms needed to understand Yarvin, NRx, and the broader reactionary movement. While many of these ideas are framed as **innovative critiques of democracy**, they often rely on **historical cherry-picking, rebranded authoritarianism, and speculative reasoning**. By understanding this terminology, readers can better engage with and critique the arguments Yarvin and his followers present.

About the Author

Hugo Rowley is the man behind Learner's Permit Guides. His appetite to learn is exceeded by hours in the day and he thought others may feel the same way - these guides are intended to help other curious people fulfill their needs.

Hugo and his family split their time between LA and Malta.

www.ingramcontent.com/pod-product-compliance
Lightning Source LLC
Chambersburg PA
CBHW021134020625
27585CB00009B/215
* 9 7 9 8 2 3 0 9 1 3 3 1 3 *